Records Management

9th Edition

Judith Read
Instructor & Department Chair
Computer Information Systems
Portland Community College
Portland, Oregon

Mary Lea Ginn, Ph.D.
Director, International Learner Services
and Institutional Review Board
Cincinnati, Ohio

SOUTH-WESTERN
CENGAGE Learning™

SOUTH-WESTERN
CENGAGE Learning™

Records Management Study Guide,
Ninth Edition
Judith Read, Mary Lea Ginn

Vice President of Editorial Director:
  Jack W. Calhoun

Vice President of Editor-in-Chief:
  Karen Schmohe

Senior Acquisitions Editor: Jane Phelan

Senior Developmental Editor:
  Penny Shank

Associate Content Project Manager:
  Jana Lewis

Marketing Manager: Laura Stopa

Manufacturing Coordinator: Kevin Kluck

Sr. Art Director: Tippy McIntosh

Consulting Editor: Dianne Rankin

Production House: S4Carlisle Publishing
  Services

Internal and Cover Designer:
  LouAnn Thesing

Cover Images: © Media Bakery

For product information and technology assistance, contact us at
Cengage Learning Customer & Sales Support, 1-800-354-9706

For permission to use material from this text or product,
submit all requests online at **www.cengage.com/permissions**
Further permissions questions can be e-mailed to
permissionrequest@cengage.com

ISBN-13: 978-0-538-73143-0
ISBN-10: 0-538-73143-5

South-Western Cengage Learning
5191 Natorp Boulevard
Mason, OH 45040
USA

Cengage Learning products are represented in Canada by Nelson Education, Ltd.

For your course and learning solutions, visit **www.cengage.com/southwestern**

Visit our company website at **www.cengage.com**

Printed in the United States of America
1 2 3 4 5 13 12 11 10

TABLE OF CONTENTS

RECORDS MANAGEMENT

Terms

Directions: Fill in the missing word(s) in the space provided at the left.

1. _external_

2. _Records Manamger_

3. _Z_

4. _Records_

5. _files_

6. _____

7. _____

8. _____

9. _____

10. _____

11. _____

12. _____

13. _____

1. Records classified by place of use are internal records and _ex_ records.

2. A permanent storage place for records is called the _____.

3. A(n) _Z_ record is used to assist in performing a firm's business operations and, if destroyed, is replaceable only at great cost.

4. _____ is an association of information management professionals.

5. Even though it may be created outside the firm, a(n) _____ record is used to store information needed to operate the firm.

6. A(n) _____ record is the least valuable of all records in a firm.

7. _____ is a communication procedure between two companies that allows the exchange of standardized documents through computers.

8. Stored information, regardless of media or characteristics, made or received by an organization that is evidence of its operations and has value requiring its retention for a specific period of time is a(n) _____.

9. The life span of a record that follows a set of phases from creation to final disposition is called the _____.

10. _____ is a system that enables users to compose, transmit, receive, and manage electronic documents and images across networks.

11. _____ is the systematic control of all records from their creation or receipt, through their processing, distribution, organization, storage, and retrieval, to their ultimate disposition.

12. _____ is an electronic method to conduct business communication and transactions over networks and through computers.

13. A group of interrelated resources—people, equipment and supplies, space, procedures, and information—acting together according to a plan to accomplish the goals of the records management program is a(n) _____.

14. _____ 14. Records that contain information needed to carry on the operations of a firm over long periods of time are _____ documents.

15. _____ 15. The _____ is a worldwide network of computers that allows public access to send, store, and receive electronic information over public networks.

16. _____ 16. _____ is a standard for records management policies and procedures.

17. _____ 17. A record that is helpful in conducting business operations and that may, if destroyed, be replaced at slight cost is a(n) _____ record.

18. _____ 18. A record used in a firm's day-to-day operations is a(n) _____ document.

19. _____ 19. _____ records must be kept permanently because they are needed for continuing the operations of a firm and are usually not replaceable.

20. _____ 20. _____ is the system and procedures that provide for electronic payments and collections.

21. _____ 21. _____ is the process of using an organization's resources to achieve specific goals through the functions of planning, organizing, leading, and controlling.

22. _____ 22. _____ is a part of the Internet that contains HTML documents that can be displayed and searched using web browser programs.

23. _____ 23. _____ describes the technologies, tools, and methods used to capture, manage, store, preserve, and deliver content across an enterprise or organization.

24. _____ 24. A(n) _____ record is a record stored on electronic media that can be readily accessed or changed.

25. _____ 25. _____ is now the primary mode of communication between employees in many corporations and governmental agencies.

True/False

Directions: Circle T if the statement is true; circle F if the statement is false.

T F   1. Only information that is handwritten or printed qualifies as a record.

T F   2. Two companies may exchange invoices or purchase orders using electronic data interchange.

T F   3. Transaction documents are records used to carry on the operations of a firm over long periods of time.

T F   4. The broad view of records as important information resources originated during the early records period—before the 1950s.

T F   5. Enterprise content management is an up-and-coming process that will benefit organizations in efficiency and effectiveness because of the combination of people, processes, and technology.

Multiple Choice

Directions: Circle the letter of the best answer.

1. Due to a number of corporate and accounting scandals, this federal law was enacted in order to enhance standards for all U.S. public company boards, management, and public accounting firms.
   a. Fair Credit Reporting Act
   b. Health Insurance Portability and Accountability Act
   c. Patriot Act
   d. Sarbanes-Oxley Act

2. During which of the following phases in the record life cycle does retrieval occur?
   a. Creation
   b. Disposition
   c. Storage
   d. Maintenance

3. Internal records may be created
   a. inside the firm only.
   b. both inside and outside the firm but for internal use.
   c. for transaction purposes only.
   d. for reference purposes only.

4. Which statement most accurately reflects the process of management?
   a. A process performed only by managers
   b. A process sometimes performed by managers and nonmanagers
   c. A process frequently performed by nonmanagers such as college students
   d. A process frequently performed by managers and nonmanagers

5. A collection of web pages on various topics that allows people who access it to contribute or modify content is a
   a. podcast.
   b. wiki.
   c. tweet.
   d. message board.

6. A shared, online journal is a
   a. podcast.
   b. wiki.
   c. tweet.
   d. blog.

Activity 1-1   Classifying Records

Directions: Place an X in the column(s) that correctly identifies(y) the appropriate classification of each record.

| Records | Records Classifications | | |
| | (a) | (b) | (c) |
	By Use	By Place of Use	By Value of Record to the Firm
Example: Bank check	X		
1. Invoices			
2. Custom refund form			
3. Articles of incorporation			
4. Filing supplies catalog			
5. Business letter			
6. Payroll record			
7. Annual picnic announcement			
8. Memo of new mailing procedures			
9. Accounts receivable record			
10. Purchase order			
11. Annual report to shareholders			
12. Yesterday's telephone messages			

Activity 1-2   Determining the Value of Records

Directions: Using the example below as a model, place an X in the column that best identifies the value of each record.

| Records | Records Value | | | |
	Administrative	Fiscal	Legal	Historical
Example: Photograph album of your business club				X
1. Income tax return				
2. Minutes of meetings				
3. Deed to property owned				
4. Title to your car				
5. Employee handbook				
6. Copy of your weekly time sheet				
7. Invoice				
8. Procedures manual				
9. Your class group graduation picture				
10. Contract to purchase a computer				

Activity 1-3   Matching Exercise

Directions: Match a statement in Column B to the appropriate term in Column A.

A

B

_____ 1. a vital record

_____ 2. fiscal value

_____ 3. World Wide Web

_____ 4. archives

_____ 5. maintenance phase

_____ 6. Freedom of Information Act

_____ 7. controlling

_____ 8. centralized

_____ 9. Privacy Act

_____ 10. leading

a. permanent storage place for records

b. storing, retrieving, and protecting records

c. a worldwide hypermedia system

d. a firm's articles of incorporation

e. training, supervising, and motivating personnel

f. involves measuring how well goals are met

g. provides the right to see information about yourself

h. provides the right to exclude others from your files

i. records are physically located and controlled in one area

j. uses of records for documenting operating funds or other financial purposes

Activity 1-4   The Record and Information Life Cycle: Phases and Activities

Directions: In each of the boxes below, write one word that identifies a phase in the record and information life cycle. On the lines provided, list two or more activities typically performed in each phase. Select answers from the textbook and from your own experiences.

1. Phases in the record and information life cycle

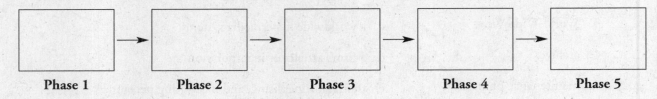

| **Phase 1** | **Phase 2** | **Phase 3** | **Phase 4** | **Phase 5** |

2. Activities typically performed in each phase of the record and information life cycle:

Phase 1: _____

Phase 2: _____

Phase 3: _____

Phase 4: _____

Phase 5: _____

Activity 1-5   Records Center Visit

Directions: List specific records activities that you would like to observe if you had an opportunity to visit a records center in your community.

1. _____

2. _____

3. _____

4. _____

5. _____

Activity 1-6   Outlining a Records Management Career Plan

Directions: Write the answers to the following items based on both information found in the textbook and your personal career interests.

1. Three sources that offer specialized information on records management are:

    a. _____

    b. _____

    c. _____

2. Four questions that I need to answer about my career interests and aptitudes are:

    a. _____

    b. _____

    c. _____

    d. _____

3. Four steps I should take to prepare for a records management career are:

    a. _____

    b. _____

    c. _____

    d. _____

SOLUTIONS

Terms

1. external
2. archives
3. important
4. ARMA International
5. internal
6. nonessential
7. electronic data interchange (EDI)
8. record
9. record and information life cycle
10. electronic mail
11. records management
12. e-commerce
13. records system
14. reference
15. Internet
16. ISO 15489
17. useful
18. transaction
19. vital
20. electronic fund transfer (EFT)
21. management
22. World Wide Web
23. enterprise content management (ECM)
24. electronic
25. e-mail

True/False

1. F
2. T
3. F
4. F
5. T

Multiple Choice

1. d
2. d
3. b
4. d
5. b
6. d

Activity 1-1   Classifying Records

1. a, b, c
2. a, c
3. c
4. a, c
5. a, b, c
6. b, c
7. b, c
8. a, b, c
9. a, b, c
10. a, b, c
11. b, c
12. c

Activity 1-2   Determining the Value of Records

1. fiscal
2. historical
3. legal
4. legal
5. administrative

6. fiscal
7. fiscal
8. administrative
9. historical
10. legal

Activity 1-3   Matching Exercise

1. d
2. j
3. c
4. a
5. b

6. g
7. f
8. i
9. h
10. e

Activity 1-4   The Record and Information Life Cycle

1. Phases in the record and information life cycle: See Figure 1.7 in the textbook for a solution to this exercise.
2. Activities typically performed in each phase of the record and information life cycle:

Phase 1 **creation:**
writing a letter; keying an e-mail; removing an incoming letter from its envelope

Phase 2 **distribution:**
picking up mail from out-boxes; placing a signed letter in an envelope and affixing postage

Phase 3 **use:**
analyzing the data appearing in a table; checking the date of a letter in a file

Phase 4 **maintenance:**
filing a record; retrieving a record from a file for use

Phase 5 **disposition:**
examining records to determine whether they are obsolete; moving old records to the archives

Activity 1-5   Records Center Visit

Student responses will vary. Some possible activities students might like to observe are:
- the classification (of records) process
- the filing of records in several kinds of equipment
- the retrieval of several types of records
- the operation of the archives
- supervisors overseeing their workers

Activity 1-6   Outlining a Records Management Career Plan

1. Responses will vary. Some possible sources of specialized information are:
   - ARMA International's *Information Management* magazine
   - *AIIM Infonomics* magazine
   - want ads in the local newspaper
   - personnel presently employed in records management positions
2. Responses will vary. Some possible questions about career interests and aptitudes are:
   - In what kind of setting—indoors or outdoors—do I prefer to work?
   - What are my short- and long-term interests as far as employment or a profession is concerned?
   - What does my school record indicate about my aptitudes and interests? For example, what elective courses have I taken and why? How well did I perform in such courses?
   - What advice can my instructors/parents/friends give me regarding my career plans?
3. Responses will vary. Some possible career steps are:
   - Study carefully the information available on such a career.
   - Determine the personal, experience, and academic requirements for each level of work in the field.
   - Talk with experienced records management personnel concerning the future of such a profession.
   - Visit a records management program in operation in a local business firm.
   - Register for courses suggested/required for work in this field.

ALPHABETIC INDEXING RULES 1–4

Terms

Directions: Fill in the missing word(s) in the space provided at the left.

1. _____

2. _____

3. _____

4. _____

5. _____

6. _____

7. _____

8. _____

9. _____

10. _____

1. The mental process of determining the filing segment (name) by which a record is to be stored and the placing or listing of items in an order that follows a particular system is called _____.

2. The first unit of a filing segment and the unit by which a record is stored is the _____.

3. When a record is requested by a name other than its originally coded name, a _____ is used to aid in retrieving that record.

4. _____ is the actual marking of a record to indicate its placement in storage.

5. The written procedures that describe how filing segments are ordered are called _____.

6. The organized way in which records are stored is called a _____.

7. The name by which a record is stored can be called a _____.

8. Personal names are in _____ order when the surname is the key unit and the given name is the second unit.

9. The various words that the filing segment contains are called the _____.

10. _____ is arranging records in the sequence in which they are to be stored.

True/False

Directions: Circle T if the statement is true; circle F if the statement is false.

T   F   1. If determining a surname is difficult in a personal name, consider the first word written as the surname.

T   F   2. In the coding process, the filer mentally determines the indexing order of the filing segment.

T   F   3. In filing alphabetically, using written rules is critical for consistent and accurate retrieval.

T   F   4. Business names are indexed exactly like personal names.

T   F   5. Symbols in business names are spelled out and considered separate indexing units.

T   F   6. The most important concept to remember is that filing is done to facilitate storing records for future use.

T   F   7. The word *the* in a business name is always considered the last indexing unit.

T   F   8. Conjunctions and prepositions are considered separate indexing units.

Multiple Choice

Directions: Circle the letter of the best answer.

1. Punctuation marks are
    a. used to separate indexing units.
    b. important for speed in retrieval.
    c. disregarded in indexing personal and business names.
    d. not used in business names.

2. Abbreviated personal names are
    a. spelled out for indexing.
    b. disregarded.
    c. combined with initials.
    d. indexed as written.

3. Single letters in business names are
    a. indexed as the last unit.
    b. indexed separately if a space separates the letters or indexed as one unit if the letters are not separated by spaces.
    c. indexed as the first unit.
    d. disregarded.

4. Circle the letter of the correct alphabetic order of the following names.

A	B
1. Roslyn N. Kale	1. Littleton Management
2. Roslyn's Fashions	2. Jennifer Jason Little
3. Kale Investment Co.	3. Littleton Coffee Corporation
4. Kale Cable TV	4. J & J Buffet
a. 2, 3, 4, 1	a. 2, 3, 1, 4
b. 4, 3, 1, 2	b. 4, 3, 2, 1
c. 4, 1, 2, 3	c. 4, 2, 3, 1
d. 4, 3, 1, 2	d. 2, 4, 3, 1

Activity 2-1   Identifying the Units in Filing Segments

1. **Directions: Write the following names in the correct indexing unit columns.**

Filing Segement	Key Unit	Unit 2	Unit 3	Unit 4
1. A Fine-Arts Preschool				
2. Beach Bum Sand Togs				
3. Lester Babb				
4. Hiroshi Abe				
5. Susan Cabe-Babb				
6. The Be-Bop Dance Studio				
7. Sandra Beach				
8. Chang Cha				
9. Debra Aaberg				
10. Holly M. Cabe				
11. A J Enterprises, Inc.				
12. Claassen & Adair Brokers				
13. J. Clarahan				
14. ABC Productions, Inc.				
15. Fred S. Asante				
16. Delores Carter				
17. Calvin E. Adair				
18. All-Away Shipping Co.				
19. The Cabana Shoppe				
20. Eun-Hee Cha				

2. Directions: Prepare any needed cross-references for names listed in No. 1.

	Original	Cross-Reference

1. _____

   _____

2. _____

   _____

3. _____

   _____

4. _____

   _____

5. _____

   _____

3. Directions: List the numbers of items 1–20 and the cross-references in alphabetic order. _____

Activity 2-2   Mystery Sentence Puzzle

Directions: Select the correct indexing unit as indicated in Column B for the names listed in Column A. Write the <u>first letter</u> of the correct indexing unit in the blank box above the corresponding number. No. 1 has been done for you. The first letter of the key unit (e) is written in the blank box above the 1. A sentence relating to records management is formed if the blanks are filled in correctly.

														e					
4	12	11	16	14	6		5	17		2	18	25		1	13	7	20		15	21

19	26	10	22	9	23	8	3	24

Column A	Column B
1. Eddy's Used Cars	Select Key Unit
2. Francis T. Dollup	Select 2nd Unit
3. Dot's Odds & Ends	Select 3rd Unit
4. Fulton's for Relaxation	Select 2nd Unit

5.	In-the-Know Agency	Select Key Unit
6.	First-Rate Gear, Inc.	Select 2nd Unit
7.	Helen A. Smithers	Select Key Unit
8.	Joan Voohees	Select Key Unit
9.	Quality, Inc.	Select 2nd Unit
10.	Tom Robinson's Tree Houses	Select 3rd Unit
11.	Financial Services of Laramie	Select 4th Unit
12.	Inez Rodriguez	Select 2nd Unit
13.	The Soto and Ludwig Law Firm	Select 2nd Unit
14.	Nona Amelio's Pizzeria	Select Key Unit
15.	Susie's Salon of Beauty	Select 3rd Unit
16.	Fred I. Alvarado	Select 3rd Unit
17.	Selected Time, Ltd.	Select Key Unit
18.	Limitless Opportunities	Select 2nd Unit
19.	Rene's Cut and Clips	Select Key Unit
20.	George Edwards	Select Key Unit
21.	Mary Anne's for Lace	Select 3rd Unit
22.	The Seaside Resort	Select 2nd Unit
23.	Energy-Dynamics Company	Select Key Unit
24.	Laptop Computer Store	Select Key Unit
25.	Melanie's Restaurant	Select 2nd Unit
26.	Read's Editorial Service	Select 2nd Unit

Activity 2-3   Coding and Arranging I

1. Directions: *Code each name by placing a diagonal between the units, underlining the key unit, and numbering succeeding units. After coding, indicate the correct alphabetic order by numbering the names 1–10 on the lines provided. An example follows.*

            2   3

Example: Marianne / D. / <u>Bethke</u>

_____ a. Lee's Wee Care Clothing

_____ b. Kuang-ping Kieu

_____ c. Lafferty & Logan Assoc.

_____ d. Denise Lee

_____ e. Keep-em Flying Flight School

_____ f. Kelly M. Baxter

_____ g. Shed #s Diet Center

_____ h. The Lark Sisters Bakery

_____ i. Leticia's House of Beauty

_____ j. Sue's Cut & Curl

2. Directions: *Code each name by placing diagonals between the units, underlining the key unit, and numbering the succeeding units. After coding, indicate the correct alphabetic order by numbering the names 1–10 on the lines provided.*

_____ k. $ Sundries, Inc.

_____ l. Day-N-Night Co.

_____ m. Verna Carson-Day

_____ n. Copies Now!

_____ o. Kayoko Baba

_____ p. Beppu & Chiba Studios

_____ q. Rinji Chiba

_____ r. Day & Wilson Law Firm

_____ s. $ Smart Savers

_____ t. Karen Davis

3. Prepare any needed cross-references for items a–t.

	Original	Cross-Reference
1.	_____	_____
		_____
2.	_____	_____
		_____
3.	_____	_____
		_____
4.	_____	_____
		_____
5.	_____	_____
		_____
6.	_____	_____
		_____
7.	_____	_____
		_____
8.	_____	_____
		_____

Activity 2-4   Coding and Arranging II

Directions: Code each name by placing a diagonal between the units, underlining the key unit, and then numbering any other units. After coding, indicate the correct alphabetic order for each set of names by putting the letters of the items in order.

1. a. Karl Szep

    b. S-Z Industries, Inc.

    c. Syrian-American Club

    d. Karl J. Szep

       Correct order _____

2. a. Larry H. Miller

    b. Miller's Pharmacy

    c. Laura Miller Repair Shop

    d. Larry R. Miller

       Correct order _____

3. a. Roberta Davis-Carter

    b. K. H. Davis

    c. Karla Davis

    d. Roberta H. Davis-Carter

       Correct order _____

4. a. Mitchell Travis

    b. Michael A. Travis

    c. Mike A. Travis

    d. Cynthia Travis-James

       Correct order _____

5. a. Rachael Pettibone

    b. R. Pettibone

    c. Rachael W. Pettibone

    d. R. W. Pettibone

       Correct order _____

6. a. Jim Smith Co.

    b. W. Smith

    c. Wayne Smith

    d. The Smith Company

       Correct order _____

Activity 2-5   Coding and Arranging III

1. **Directions: Code the following personal and business names by placing a diagonal between units, underlining the key unit, and numbering the remaining units. Then alphabetize the names by numbering them 1–24 on the lines provided.**

_____ a. TLC Child Care

_____ b. T&C Fabricating Company

_____ c. TRS (Total Residential Service)

_____ d. S-Mart Cars, Inc.

_____ e. Rest Awhile Motel

_____ f. John Rosen

_____ g. Tunney & Rosen Brokerage

_____ h. Taylor's Multimedia Productions

_____ i. Redi Form Printing

_____ j. Melissa Taylor

_____ k. Marissa Reid-Tyler

_____ l. Residential Bio-Quip, Inc.

_____ m. The Superior Card Shop

_____ n. R L Q Gifts & Toys

_____ o. Ronald Reston

_____ p. Elizabeth Schwab

_____ q. Sav-On Car Rental

_____ r. Elizabeth Schwaub

_____ s. Phillip Raad

_____ t. Lydia Taylorson

_____ u. Dan Tunney

_____ v. Redi-Form Service, Inc.

_____ w. Smart Service, Inc.

_____ x. Dan B. Tunney

2. **Directions: Prepare any needed cross-references for items a–x.**

Original	Cross-Reference
1. _____	_____
	_____
2. _____	_____
	_____
3. _____	_____
	_____

SOLUTIONS

Terms

1. indexing
2. key unit
3. cross-reference
4. coding
5. indexing rules
6. filing (or storing) method
7. filing segment
8. indexing
9. indexing units
10. sorting

True/False

1. F
2. F
3. T
4. F
5. T
6. F
7. F
8. T

Multiple Choice

1. c
2. d
3. b
4a. d (4, 3, 1, 2)
4b. c (4, 2, 3, 1)

Activity 2-1   Identifying the Units in Filing Segments

1. Correct indexing order

Filing Segement	Key Unit	Unit 2	Unit 3	Unit 4
1. A Fine-Arts Preschool	A	FineArts	Preschool	
2. Beach Bum Sand Togs	Beach	Bum	Sand	Togs
3. Lester Babb	Babb	Lester		
4. Hiroshi Abe	Abe	Hiroshi		
5. Susan Cabe-Babb	CabeBabb	Susan		
6. The Be-Bop Dance Studio	BeBop	Dance	Studio	The

Filing Segement	Key Unit	Unit 2	Unit 3	Unit 4
7. Sandra Beach	Beach	Sandra		
8. Chang Cha	Cha	Chang		
9. Debra Aaberg	Aaberg	Debra		
10. Holly M. Cabe	Cabe	Holly	M	
11. A J Enterprises, Inc.	A	J	Enterprises	Inc
12. Claassen & Adair Brokers	Claassen	and	Adair	Brokers
13. J. Clarahan	Clarahan	J		
14. ABC Productions, Inc.	ABC	Productions	Inc	
15. Fred S. Asante	Asante	Fred	S	
16. Delores Carter	Carter	Delores		
17. Calvin E. Adair	Adair	Calvin	E	
18. All-Away Shipping Co.	AllAway	Shipping	Co	
19. The Cabana Shoppe	Cabana	Shoppe	The	
20. Eun-Hee Cha	Cha	EunHee		

2. Cross-references for items 1–20

Original	Cross-Reference
4. Abe Hiroshi	Hiroshi Abe
	SEE Abe Hiroshi
5. CabeBabb Susan	Babb Susan Cabe
	SEE CabeBabb Susan
8. Cha Chang	Chang Cha
	SEE Cha Chang
12. Claassen and Adair Brokers	Adair and Claassen Brokers
	SEE Claassen and Adair Brokers
20. Cha EunHee	EunHee Cha
	SEE Cha EunHee

3. The correct order is: <u>1, 11, 9, 14, 4, 12X, 17, 18, 15, 3, 5X, 2, 7, 6, 19, 10, 5, 16, 8, 20, 8X, 12, 13, 20X, 4X</u>

Activity 2-2   Mystery Sentence Puzzle

The sentence is ***filing is for ease of retrieval.***

Activity 2-3   Coding and Arranging I

1. Coding and correct alphabetic order

               2   3   4
<u> 7 </u> a. <u>Lee's</u> / Wee / Care / Clothing

               2
<u> 3 </u> b. Kuang-ping / <u>Kieu</u>

               2   3   4
<u> 4 </u> c. <u>Lafferty</u> / & / Logan / Assoc.

               2
<u> 6 </u> d. Denise / <u>Lee</u>

               2   3   4
<u> 2 </u> e. <u>Keep-em</u> / Flying / Flight / School

               2   3
<u> 1 </u> f. Kelly / M. / <u>Baxter</u>

               2   3   4
<u> 9 </u> g. <u>Shed</u> / #s / Diet / Center

               4   2   3
<u> 5 </u> h. The / <u>Lark</u> / Sisters / Bakery

               2   3   4
<u> 8 </u> i. <u>Leticia's</u> / House / of / Beauty

               2   3   4
<u>10</u> j. <u>Sue's</u> / Cut / & / Curl

2. Coding and correct alphabetic order

               2   3
<u>10</u> k. <u>$</u> / Sundries, / Inc.

               2
<u> 8 </u> l. <u>Day-N-Night</u> / Co.

               2
<u> 3 </u> m. Verna / <u>Carson-Day</u>

               2
<u> 5 </u> n. <u>Copies</u> / Now!

               2
<u> 1 </u> o. Kayoko / <u>Baba</u>

               2   3   4
<u> 2 </u> p. <u>Beppu</u> / & / Chiba / Studios

               2
<u> 4 </u> q. Rinji / <u>Chiba</u>

               2   3   4   5
<u> 7 </u> r. <u>Day</u> / & / Wilson / Law / Firm

               2   3
<u> 9 </u> s. <u>$</u> / Smart / Savers

               2
<u> 6 </u> t. Karen / <u>Davis</u>

3. Cross-references for items a–t

Original	Cross-Reference

b. Kieu Kuangping — Kuangping Kieu

SEE Kieu Kuangping

c. Lafferty and Logan Assoc — Logan and Lafferty Assoc

SEE Lafferty and Logan Assoc

m. CarsonDay Verna — Day Verna Carson

SEE CarsonDay Verna

o. Baba Kayoko — Kayoko Baba

SEE Baba Kayoko

p. Beppu and Chiba Studios — Chiba and Beppu Studios

SEE Beppu and Chiba Studios

q. Chiba Rinji — Rinji Chiba

SEE Chiba Rinji

r. Day and Wilson Law Firm — Wilson and Day Law Firm

SEE Day and Wilson Law Firm

Activity 2-4   Coding and Arranging II

1. a. Karl / <u>Szep</u>
      ²

   b. <u>S-Z</u> / Industries, / Inc.

   c. <u>Syrian-American</u> / Club

   d. Karl / J. / <u>Szep</u>

   Correct order <u>c, b, a, d</u>

2. a. Larry / H. / <u>Miller</u>

   b. <u>Miller's</u> / Pharmacy

   c. <u>Laura</u> / Miller / Repair / Shop

   d. Larry / R. / <u>Miller</u>

   Correct order <u>c, a, d, b</u>

3. a. Roberta / <u>Davis-Carter</u>

   b. K. / H. / <u>Davis</u>

   c. Karla / <u>Davis</u>

   d. Roberta / H. / <u>Davis-Carter</u>

   Correct order <u>b, c, a, d</u>

4. a. Mitchell / <u>Travis</u>

   b. Michael / A. / <u>Travis</u>

   c. Mike / A. / <u>Travis</u>

   d. Cynthia / <u>Travis-James</u>

   Correct order <u>b, c, a, d</u>

5. a. Rachael / <u>Pettibone</u>

   b. R. / <u>Pettibone</u>

   c. Rachael / W. / <u>Pettibone</u>

   d. R. / W. / <u>Pettibone</u>

   Correct order <u>b, d, a, c</u>

6. a. <u>Jim</u> / Smith / Co.

   b. W. / <u>Smith</u>

   c. Wayne / <u>Smith</u>

   d. The / <u>Smith</u> / Company

   Correct order <u>a, d, b, c</u>

Activity 2-5   Coding and Arranging III

1. Coding and correct alphabetic order

   _20_ a. <u>TLC</u> / Child / Care

   _16_ b. <u>T&C</u> / Fabricating / Company

   _21_ c. <u>TRS</u> (Total Residential Service)

   _13_ d. <u>S-Mart</u> / Cars, / Inc.

   _7_ e. <u>Rest</u> / Awhile / Motel

   _9_ f. John / <u>Rosen</u>

   _22_ g. <u>Tunney</u> / & / Rosen / Brokerage

   _18_ h. <u>Taylor's</u> / Multimedia / Productions

		2	3			

  3   i. Re<u>di</u> / Form / Printing

  17   j. Melissa / <u>Taylor</u>

  5   k. Marissa / <u>Reid-Tyler</u>

  6   l. <u>Residential</u> / Bio-Quip, / Inc.

  15   m. The / <u>Superior</u> / Card / Shop

  1   n. <u>R</u> / L / Q / Gifts / & / Toys

  8   o. Ronald / <u>Reston</u>

  11   p. Elizabeth / <u>Schwab</u>

  10   q. <u>Sav-On</u> / Car / Rental

  12   r. Elizabeth / <u>Schwaub</u>

  2   s. Phillip / <u>Raad</u>

  19   t. Lydia / <u>Taylorson</u>

  23   u. Dan / <u>Tunney</u>

  4   v. <u>Redi-Form</u> / Service, / Inc.

  14   w. <u>Smart</u> / Service, / Inc.

  24   x. Dan / B. / <u>Tunney</u>

2. Cross-references for items a–x

Original	**Cross-Reference**
c. TRS	Total Residential Service
	SEE TRS
g. Tunney and Rosen Brokerage	Rosen and Tunney Brokerage
	SEE Tunney and Rosen Brokerage
k. ReidTyler Marissa	Tyler Marissa Reid
	SEE ReidTyler Marissa

ALPHABETIC INDEXING RULES 5–8

True/False

Directions: Circle T if the statement is true; circle F if the statement is false.

T   F   1. Business names with titles are indexed as written.

T   F   2. Articles and particles of names are treated as separate indexing units.

T   F   3. A title before a personal name is considered the key unit.

T   F   4. Names with numbers are filed under *N*.

T   F   5. Even if a company changes its name, new files are still placed under the old name.

Multiple Choice

Directions: Circle the letter of the best answer.

1. The third unit in the name Mrs. Anne Chabon, MD is
   a. Anne.
   b. MD.
   c. Mrs.
   d. Chabon.

2. The third unit in the business name Dr. Chabon's Medical Supply is
   a. Chabon's.
   b. Dr.
   c. Medical.
   d. Supply.

3. AtlCo is a division of the Atlantic Corporation. A cross-reference is prepared for
   a. Atlantic Corporation.
   b. AtlCo.
   c. AtlCo and Atlantic Corporation.
   d. No cross-reference is needed.

4. Circle the letter of the correct alphabetic order of the following names.

A
1. Allstate Hotel
2. Atlantic Aerospace
3. Atlanta Art Museum
4. Atlanta Times
   a. 1, 3, 4, 2
   b. 1, 3, 2, 4
   c. 1, 2, 3, 4
   d. 1, 2, 4, 3

B
1. Major Colleen Jarvis
2. Ms. Colleen M. Jarvis, CPA
3. Dr. Colleen M. Jarvis
4. Mr. Colin Jarvin
   a. 3, 2, 4, 1
   b. 4, 1, 2, 3
   c. 1, 2, 3, 4
   d. 4, 2, 3, 1

Activity 3-1   Identifying the Units in Filing Segments

1. Directions: Write the following names in the correct indexing unit columns.

Filing Segment	Key Unit	Unit 2	Unit 3	Unit 4
1. Mr. Joel B. Shaw				
2. Tuality General Hospital				
3. Ms. Cecilia Shelton				
4. Mrs. Elaine Teague				
5. Rio Grande Games				
6. Teamsters Joint Council				
7. Napa Valley Water				
8. Bavarian Motor Works				
9. Shear Impressions				
10. Stereophonics Recording Co.				
11. Martin Skinner, MD				
12. Michael Tso				
13. Skybridge Construction Co.				
14. Interactive Digital Communications				
15. 81st & Tacoma Café				
16. Simply Divine Desserts				
17. Seattle's Best Coffee				
18. 377 Tudor Arms Apts.				
19. William King, Jr.				
20. 1 TechWiz.Com				

2. Directions: List the numbers of items 1–20 to indicate correct alphabetic order. _____

Activity 3-2   Coding and Arranging I

1. *Directions: Code each name by placing a diagonal between the units, underlining the key unit, and numbering succeeding units. After coding, indicate the correct alphabetic order by numbering the names 1–16 on the lines provided.*

_____ a. Barbara Larson-Miller

_____ b. McKinna Airlines

_____ c. Wan Hoi Lee

_____ d. Lou Mason Tires

_____ e. Luke Haines

_____ f. Coastal Royal Hotel

_____ g. La Prima Catering

_____ h. Hopper Athletics

_____ i. 1st Baptist Church

_____ j. LaRumba Restaurant

_____ k. Luke Haines, Sr.

_____ l. Carole Le Vanda, MD

_____ m. First National Bank

_____ n. Lacrosse International

_____ o. Lady Fingers Systems
       (a div. of LaSalle Management)

_____ p. 24/7 Security, Inc.

2. *Directions: Prepare needed cross-references for items a–p.*

	Original	Cross-Reference
1.	_____	_____
		_____
2.	_____	_____
		_____
3.	_____	_____
		_____

Activity 3-3   Coding and Arranging II

Directions: Code each name by placing a diagonal between the units, underlining the key unit, and numbering succeeding units. After coding, indicate the correct alphabetic order for each set of names by putting the letters of the items in order.

1. a. Managerial Systems

    b. My-T-Fine Fabrics

    c. M. Emery Walsh

    d. Motion Picture Association

    Correct order _____

2. a. Theo de Boer

    b. T. D. De Boer

    c. Theodore Deboer

    d. Ted de Boer

    Correct order _____

3. a. Uniforms for Life Co.

    b. United Baggage Handles

    c. Union Workers of America

    d. Union of Assembly Workers

    Correct order _____

4. a. Robot Manufacturing Corp

    b. Radio Free Europe

    c. R-H NewsCorp

    d. R H International

    Correct order _____

5. a. Key West Bank

    b. Key Investment Properties, Inc.

    c. Key Strategies Co.

    d. Key Hole Closets 2-Go!

    Correct order _____

6. a. 205 Shoppers Mall, Inc.

    b. 48 Doughnuts 2-Go

    c. 1 Main Place

    d. 22nd Century Products

    Correct order _____

Activity 3-4   Mystery Phrase Puzzle

Directions: Select the correct indexing unit as indicated in Column B for the names listed in Column A. Write the first letter of the correct indexing unit in the blank box above the corresponding number. No. 1 has been done for you. The first letter of the second unit (e) is written in the blank box above the 1. A phrase relating to records management is formed if the blanks are filled in correctly.

																		e				
17	6	12	21	13	9	3		5	2	7	19	10	16		15	14	11	1	18	22	4	8	20

	A	B
1.	YMCA Educational Division	Second Unit
2.	Dr. C. Edward Yaden	Third Unit
3.	Gates Garden Plants	Second Unit
4.	U & I Travel Service	Third Unit
5.	Bernard C. Yost	Second Unit
6.	Ye Olde Town Crier	Second Unit
7.	Youth for a Greener America	Second Unit
8.	Bear Necessities, Inc.	Second Unit
9.	Daniel Nolanski	Key Unit
10.	All-Natural Health Researchers	Third Unit
11.	Thomas & Miller, Attorneys	Third Unit
12.	Tree House Café	Key Unit
13.	Interstate Promotions	Key Unit
14.	Original Hair Design	Key Unit
15.	Arthur S. McDonald	Third Unit
16.	Initially Yours Etching	Third Unit
17.	National Association for Philanthropy	Key Unit
18.	Time for Flowers	Key Unit
19.	Our Savior Baptist Church	Key Unit
20.	G. A. Salizar	Second Unit
21.	National Health Association	Second Unit
22.	Orchid Growers Association of Hawaii	Fifth Unit

Activity 3-5   Coding and Arranging III

1. **Directions:** *Code each name by placing a diagonal between the units, underlining the key unit, and numbering succeeding units. After coding, indicate the correct alphabetic order by numbering the names 1–10 on the lines provided.*

_____ a. Stump Town Café

_____ b. St. Paul Lutheran Church

_____ c. Mrs. Margaret Stamps, Ph.D.

_____ d. 77 Sunset Strip, Inc.

_____ e. Students for Ending Hunger

_____ f. 405 Engine Repair Co.

_____ g. The Statesman-Journal, Inc.

_____ h. Strategy 1 Company

_____ i. Samson's Hair Care

_____ j. Stamp Collecting Association

2. **Directions:** *Code each name by placing a diagonal between the units, underlining the key unit, and numbering the succeeding units. After coding, indicate the correct alphabetic order by numbering the names 1–14 on the lines provided.*

_____ k. Nabisco, Inc. (a div. of Kraft Foods, Inc.)

_____ l. Ms. Amber Garman, CRM

_____ m. Good Will Organization

_____ n. Nextel, Inc.
(changed name from New Cell, Inc.)

_____ o. Mrs. Susan Norris, CPA

_____ p. Nu-to-You Shoppe

_____ q. Peter St. Claire DVM

_____ r. Grandma's Restaurant

_____ s. #1 Sports Stop

_____ t. Gunther's Auto Parts

_____ u. Global Peace Society
(popular name: Global Peace)

_____ v. Admiral George Neal

_____ w. South East Video Games

_____ x. Stein, Sills, and Uhl Jewelers

3. **Directions:** *Prepare any needed cross-references for items a–x.*

Original	Cross-Reference
1. _____	_____
	_____
2. _____	_____
	_____
3. _____	_____
	_____

4. _____

   _____

5. _____

   _____

6. _____

   _____

7. _____

   _____

SOLUTIONS

True/False

1. T
2. F
3. F
4. F
5. F

Multiple Choice

1. b
2. c
3. a
4a. a (1, 3, 4, 2)
4b. d (4, 2, 3, 1)

Activity 3-1   Identifying the Units in Filing Segments

1. Correct indexing order

Filing Segement	Key Unit	Unit 2	Unit 3	Unit 4
1. Mr. Joel B. Shaw	Shaw	Joel	B	Mr
2. Tuality General Hospital	Tuality	General	Hospital	
3. Ms. Cecilia Shelton	Shelton	Cecilia	Ms	
4. Mrs. Elaine Teague	Teague	Elaine	Mrs	
5. Rio Grande Games	Rio	Grande	Games	
6. Teamsters Joint Council	Teamsters	Joint	Council	
7. Napa Valley Water	Napa	Valley	Water	
8. Bavarian Motor Works	Bavarian	Motor	Works	
9. Shear Impressions	Shear	Impressions		
10. Stereophonics Recording Co.	Stereophonics	Recording	Co	
11. Martin Skinner, MD	Skinner	Martin	MD	
12. Michael Tso	Tso	Michael		
13. Skybridge Construction Co.	Skybridge	Construction	Co	

Filing Segement	Key Unit	Unit 2	Unit 3	Unit 4
14. Interactive Digital Communications	Interactive	Digital	Communications	
15. 81st & Tacoma Café	81	and	Tacoma	Cafe
16. Simply Divine Desserts	Simply	Divine	Desserts	
17. Seattle's Best Coffee	Seattles	Best	Coffee	
18. 377 Tudor Arms Apts.	377	Tudor	Arms	Apts
19. William King, Jr.	King	William	Jr	
20. 1 TechWiz.Com	1	TechWizcom		

2. The correct order is:

   20, 15, 18, 8, 14, 19, 7, 5, 17, 1, 9, 3, 16, 11, 13, 10, 4, 6, 12, 2

Activity 3-2   Coding and Arranging I

1. Coding and correct alphabetic order

             2
__11__ a. Barbara / <u>Larson-Miller</u>

             2
__16__ b. <u>McKinna</u> / Airlines

             2   3
__13__ c. Wan / Hoi / <u>Lee</u>

             2   3
__15__ d. <u>Lou</u> / Mason / Tires

             2
__5__ e. Luke / <u>Haines</u>

             2   3
__3__ f. <u>Coastal</u> / Royal / Hotel

             2
__10__ g. La Prima / Catering

             2
__7__ h. <u>Hopper</u> / Athletics

             2   3
__1__ i. <u>1st</u> / Baptist / Church

             2
__12__ j. <u>LaRumba</u> / Restaurant

             2   3
__6__ k. Luke / <u>Haines,</u> / Sr.

             2   3
__14__ l. Carole / <u>Le Vanda,</u> / MD

             2   3
__4__ m. <u>First</u> / National / Bank

             2
__8__ n. <u>Lacrosse</u> / International

             2   3
__9__ o. <u>Lady</u> / Fingers / Systems
               (a div. of LaSalle Management)

             2   3
__2__ p. <u>24/7</u> / Security, / Inc.

2. Cross-references for items a–p

	Original	Cross-Reference
a.	LarsonMiller Barbara	Miller Barbara Larson
		SEE LarsonMiller Barbara
c.	Lee Wan Hoi	Wan Hoi Lee
		SEE Lee Wan Hoi
o.	Lady Fingers Systems	LaSalle Management
		SEE Lady Finger Systems

Activity 3-3   Coding and Arranging II

1.
              2
 a. <u>Managerial</u> / Systems
              2
 b. <u>My-T-Fine</u> / Fabrics
      2   3
 c. <u>M.</u> / Emery / <u>Walsh</u>
         2   3
 d. <u>Motion</u> / Picture / Association
 Correct order <u>a, d, b, c</u>

2.
              2
 a. Theo / <u>de Boer</u>
      2   3
 b. T. / D. / <u>De Boer</u>
         2
 c. Theodore / <u>Deboer</u>
         2
 d. Ted / <u>de Boer</u>
 Correct order <u>b, d, a, c</u>

3.
          2   3   4
 a. <u>Uniforms</u> / for / Life / Co.
          2   3
 b. <u>United</u> / Baggage / Handlers
         2   3   4
 c. <u>Union</u> / Workers / of / America
        2   3   4
 d. <u>Union</u> / of / Assembly / Workers
 Correct order <u>a, d, c, b</u>

4.
         2   3
 a. <u>Robot</u> / Manufacturing / Corp
         2   3
 b. <u>Radio</u> / Free / Europe
         2
 c. <u>R-H</u> / NewsCorp
      2   3
 d. <u>R</u> / H / International
 Correct order <u>d, b, c, a</u>

5.
         2   3
 a. <u>Key</u> / West / Bank
         2   3   4
 b. <u>Key</u> / Investment / Properties, / Inc.
         2   3
 c. <u>Key</u> / Strategies / Co.
         2   3   4
 d. <u>Key</u> / Hole / Closets / 2-Go!
 Correct order <u>d, b, c, a</u>

6.
         2   3   4
 a. <u>205</u> / Shoppers / Mall, / Inc.
         2   3
 b. <u>48</u> / Doughnuts / 2-Go
         2   3
 c. <u>1</u> / Main / Place
         2   3
 d. <u>22nd</u> / Century / Products
 Correct order <u>c, d, b, a</u>

Activity 3-4   Mystery Phrase Puzzle

The phrase is *nothing before something.*

Activity 3-5   Coding and Arranging III

1. Coding and correct alphabetic order

		2 3
10	a.	Stump / Town / Café

		2 3
7	b.	St. Paul / Lutheran / Church

		4 2 3
5	c.	Mrs. / Margaret / Stamps, / Ph.D.

		2 3 4
1	d.	77 / Sunset / Strip, / Inc.

		2 3 4
9	e.	Students / for / Ending / Hunger

		2 3 4
2	f.	405 / Engine / Repair / Co.

		3 2
6	g.	The / Statesman-Journal, / Inc.

		2 3
8	h.	Strategy / 1 / Company

		2 3
3	i.	Samson's / Hair / Care

		2 3
4	j.	Stamp / Collecting / Association

2. Coding and correct alphabetic order

		2
6	k.	Nabisco, / Inc.
		(a div. of Kraft Foods, Inc.)

		4 2 3
1	l.	Ms. / Amber / Garman, / CRM

		2 3
3	m.	Good / Will / Organization

		2
8	n.	Nextel, / Inc.
		(changed name from New Cell, Inc.)

		4 2 3
9	o.	Mrs. / Susan / Norris, / CPA

		2
11	p.	Nu-to-You / Shoppe

		2 3
13	q.	Peter / St. Claire / DVM

		2
4	r.	Grandma's / Restaurant

		2 3
10	s.	#1 / Sports / Stop

		2 3
5	t.	Gunther's / Auto / Parts

		2 3
2	u.	Global / Peace / Society
		(popular name: Global Peace)

		3 2
7	v.	Admiral / George / Neal

		2 3 4
12	w.	South / East / Video / Games

		2 3 4 5
14	x.	Stein, / Sills, / and / Uhl / Jewelers

3. Cross-references for items a–x

	Original	**Cross-Reference**
k.	Nabisco Inc	Kraft Foods Inc
		SEE Nabisco Inc
m.	Good Will Organization	Goodwill
		SEE ALSO Good Will
n.	Nextel Inc	New Cell Inc
		SEE Nextel Inc
u.	Global Peace Society	Global Peace
		SEE Global Peace Society
w.	South East Video Games	Southeast
		SEE ALSO South East
x.	Stein Sills and Uhl Jewelers	Sills Uhl and Stein Jewelers
		SEE Stein Sills and Uhl Jewelers
x.	Stein Sills and Uhl Jewelers	Uhl Stein and Sills Jewelers
		SEE Stein Sills and Uhl Jewelers

ALPHABETIC INDEXING RULES 9–10

True/False

Directions: Circle T if the statement is true; circle F if the statement is false.

T   F   1. If a number is spelled out in a business name, it is filed alphabetically.
T   F   2. ZIP Codes are not considered in determining filing order.
T   F   3. If two names are identical, the state name in the address is considered next for indexing.
T   F   4. The first indexing unit of local or regional government names is the name of the department.
T   F   5. The first level of federal government names is *United States Government*.

Multiple Choice

Directions: Circle the letter of the best answer.

1. For state and local governments, *State of*, *County of*, and *City of* are
   a. not included in the indexed name.
   b. always included in the indexed name.
   c. often included for clarity.
   d. an important unit in the name.

2. If correspondence is received from a foreign government and the letterhead is written in the foreign language, a reference for finding the English spelling is
   a. an atlas.
   b. the *World Almanac and Book of Facts*.
   c. *United States Government Manual*.
   d. *IRS World Factoids*.

3. When indexing names with numbers written in digit form that contain *st* or *nd* (e.g., 2nd Hand News),
   a. write out the number.
   b. ignore the letter endings and consider only the digit.
   c. consider the filing segment as written.
   d. spell out the number.

4. Circle the letter of the correct alphabetic order of the following names.

A

1. Douglas County Sheriff's Office
2. Library Services of Douglas County
3. Douglas County Court
4. Human Services, Douglas County
   a. 3, 4, 2, 1
   b. 1, 3, 2, 4
   c. 3, 2, 1, 4
   d. 3, 2, 4, 1

B

1. Janet Stevens, Independence, Missouri
2. Janet Stevens, Independence, Oregon
3. Janet Stevens, Independence, Colorado
4. Janet Stevens, Independence, Arkansas
   a. 3, 2, 4, 1
   b. 4, 3, 1, 2
   c. 4, 2, 1, 3
   d. 4, 2, 3, 1

Activity 4-1   Federal Government Names

1. **Directions: Identify the levels (beginning with Level 2) in the filing segments below. In all cases,** United States Government *is Level 1.*

Filing Segment	Level 1: United States Government	
Name	Level 2	Level 3
1. Political Affairs, Department of State		
2. Bureau of Economic Analysis, Department of Commerce		
3. Federal Bureau of Investigation, Department of Justice		
4. Arms Control and International Security, Department of State		
5. National Marine Fisheries Service, Department of Commerce		
6. Office of English Language Acquisition, Department of Education		
7. Democracy and Global Affairs, Department of State		
8. National Communication System, Department of Homeland Security		
9. National Weather Service, Department of Commerce		
10. Drug Enforcement Administration, Department of Justice		

2. **Directions: List the numbers of items 1–10 in correct alphabetic order.** _____

Activity 4-2   Coding and Arranging I

1. Directions: *Code each name by placing a diagonal between the units, underlining the key unit, and numbering succeeding units. After coding, indicate the correct alphabetic order for each set of names by putting the letters of the items in order.*

1. a. 1700s Antiques
    b. 170 Flavors Ice Cream Shop
    c. 500 Fortune Investments
    d. 174th Street Market
    Correct order _____

2. a. Richard Davis, Dayton, Nevada
    b. Richard Davis, Dayton, Wyoming
    c. Richard Davis, Dayton, Idaho
    d. Richard Davis, Daytona, Florida
    Correct order _____

3. a. Idaho Department of Agriculture
    b. Governor's Office, State of Idaho
    c. Idaho Division of Motor Vehicles
    d. Idaho Department of Environmental Quality
    Correct order _____

4. a. 6th Avenue Pizza
    b. Sixth Street Secondhand
    c. 600 Flowers
    d. 16 Flags Parks
    Correct order _____

5. a. Dexter County Bureau of Licenses
    b. City of Dexter Municipal Library
    c. Dexter City Hall
    d. Dexter County Circuit Court
    Correct order _____

6. a. Kypriaki Dimokratia (Greek) and Kibris Cumhuriyeti (Turkish) (Republic of Cyprus)
    b. République du Tchad (Republic of Chad)
    c. República de Cabo Verde (Republic of Cape Verde)
    d. Kampuchea (Kingdom of Cambodia)
    Correct order _____

2. Directions: *Prepare needed cross-references for No. 6 above.*

	Original	Cross-Reference
1.	_____	_____
2.	_____	_____
3.	_____	_____
4.	_____	_____
5.	_____	_____

Activity 4-3   Coding and Arranging II

1. Directions: *Code each name by placing a diagonal between the units, underlining the key unit, and numbering succeeding units. After coding, indicate the correct alphabetic order for each set of names by putting the letters of the items in order.*

1. a. Vantage Point Spa
        2d Avenue
        Raleigh, North Carolina

    b. Van Delivery Service

    c. Vantage Point Spa
        31st Street
        Erie, Pennsylvania

    d. Mrs. Melinda R. Van Arsdale

    e. Vantage Point Spa
        Eastern Parkway
        Blacksburg, Virginia

        Correct order _____

2. a. Country Kitchen
        34th Avenue
        Newark, New Jersey

    b. 22nd Street Photo Lab

    c. Country Kitchen
        18th Street
        Newark, New Jersey

    d. 10 Little Indians Day Care

    e. Country Kitchen
        First Avenue
        Newark, New Jersey

        Correct order _____

3. a. Admiral Girard T. Schulte

    b. Schueler-Dillworth Designs

    c. Muriel Schumacher

    d. Heather Schuman-Lee

    e. The Schuman Education Center

        Correct order _____

4. a. Eaton City Water Works

    b. City of Etna Department of Health

    c. Pasadena Public Library

    d. Pinellas County Historical Society

    e. Eaton City Hall

        Correct order _____

2. Directions: *Prepare needed cross-references for No. 3 above.*

Original	Cross-Reference
1. _____	_____
	_____
2. _____	_____
	_____

Activity 4-4   Mystery Sentence Puzzle

Directions: Select the correct indexing unit as indicated in Column B for the names listed in Column A. Write the first letter of the correct indexing unit in the blank box above the corresponding number. No. 1 has been done for you. The first letter of the third unit (l) is written in the blank box above the 1. A sentence relating to records management is formed if the blanks are filled in correctly.

			l											
4	15	8	11	1		6	14	3		9	13	2	5	10	7	12

A	**B**
1. Mr. Jeffery Layton Simmons, CRM	Third Unit
2. State Library of Missouri	Key Unit
3. Tennessee State Patrol	Key Unit
4. St. Theresa Chapel	Key Unit
5. Ms. Jill Brown, Salem, Massachusetts	Key Unit
6. R E O Speedsters, Inc.	Third Unit
7. Lila's Lovely Things	Second Unit
8. Earnestly Yours!	Key Unit
9. Department of Tourism, State of South Dakota	Key Unit
10. Ms. Jill Brown, Salem, Oregon	Fifth Unit
11. Lubbock City Hall, Lubbock, Texas	Key Unit
12. Utah State Police	Second Unit
13. Miss Yasmine Fromdahl, RN	Second Unit
14. National Weather Service (federal government)	Level 1
15. Philip T. Norberg	Second Unit

Activity 4-5   Coding and Arranging County Names

Directions: The following government services are provided by Marion County. Code each of the items by placing a diagonal between the units, underlining the key unit, and numbering succeeding units. (Begin numbering with Unit 3; assume that the first two units are Marion, County.) Finally, alphabetize the items by numbering from 1–14 on the lines provided.

_____ 1. Administration Services, Motor Pool, Transportation Department

_____ 2. Aging Agency, Social Services Division, Human Services Department

_____ 3. Well Child Clinics, Public Health Division, Human Services Department

_____ 4. Operations and Administration, Transportation Department

_____ 5. Crime Analysis, Sheriff's Department

_____ 6. Public Library

_____ 7. Marriage Licenses, Clerk's Office

_____ 8. Budget Office, Treasurer

_____ 9. Land Use Planning, Planning Services, Transportation Department

_____ 10. Service District No. 1, Utilities Department

_____ 11. 911 Coordinator, General Service Department

_____ 12. Housing Authority, Human Services Department

_____ 13. Traffic, Sheriff's Department

_____ 14. Personnel Office, Human Resources Department

Activity 4-6   Coding and Arranging by Subject

Directions: You work in the human resources office of Geiger Pharmaceutical Industries. The company currently has openings for the following positions: Records Clerk, Records Supervisor, and Accounting Clerk. Your task is to use the following list to prepare an alphabetic listing of the positions and the names of applicants on file. In all cases, the key unit is Applications. If you have access to a computer, you may use it to prepare the listing.

The following people have applied for the position of **Records Clerk:**

Thao Nguyen	Gene Burns
Doreen Miller	Mark Smith
Susan Clarke	Clara Woods

The following people have applied for the position of **Records Supervisor:**

Lila Dodd	Beatriz Del Gado
Al-Seyed Mostifavi	Kelly Jones
Verna Moore	Samuel McDowell

The following people have applied for the position of **Accounting Clerk:**

Erika Heider	Cherie Sheng
Anita Ridgway	Linda Norton
Mike Bernstein	Akeo Yukimura
Janelle Minten	Florendo Ruiz

SOLUTIONS

True/False

1. T
2. T
3. F
4. F
5. T

Multiple Choice

1. c
2. b
3. b
4a. a (3, 4, 2, 1)
4b. b (4, 3, 1, 2)

Activity 4-1   Federal Government Names

1. Correct indexing order

Filing Segment	Level 1: United States Government	
Name	Level 2	Level 3
1. Political Affairs, Department of State	State Department (of)	Political Affairs
2. Bureau of Economic Analysis, Department of Commerce	Commerce Department (of)	Economic Analysis Bureau (of)
3. Federal Bureau of Investigation, Department of Justice	Justice Department (of)	Investigation Federal Bureau (of)
4. Arms Control and International Security, Department of State	State Department (of)	Arms Control and International Security
5. National Marine Fisheries Service, Department of Commerce	Commerce Department (of)	National Marine Fisheries Service
6. Office of English Language Acquisition, Department of Education	Education Department (of)	English Language Acquisition Office (of)
7. Democracy and Global Affairs, Department of State	State Department (of)	Democracy and Global Affairs
8. National Communication System, Department of Homeland Security	Homeland Security Department (of)	National Communication System
9. National Weather Service, Department of Commerce	Commerce Department (of)	National Weather Service
10. Drug Enforcement Administration, Department of Justice	Justice Department (of)	Drug Enforcement Administration

2. Correct order: 2, 5, 9, 6, 8, 10, 3, 4, 7, 1

Activity 4-2   Coding and Arranging I

1. a.   2
    <u>1700s</u> / Antiques
        2   3   4   5
   b. <u>170</u> / Flavors / Ice / Cream / Shop
        2   3
   c. <u>500</u> / Fortune / Investments
        2   3
   d. <u>174th</u> / Street / Market
     Correct order <u>b, d, c, a</u>

2. a.   2   3   4
    Richard / <u>Davis,</u> / Dayton, / Nevada
       2   3   4
   b. Richard / <u>Davis,</u> / Dayton, / Wyoming
       2   3   4
   c. Richard / <u>Davis,</u> / Dayton, / Idaho
       2   3   4
   d. Richard / <u>Davis,</u> / Daytona, / Florida
     Correct order <u>c, a, b, d</u>

3. a.   3   4   2
    <u>Idaho</u> / Department / of / Agriculture
        4   5   2   3
   b. Governor's / Office, / State / of / <u>Idaho</u>
           4   5   2   3
   c. <u>Idaho</u> / Division / of / Motor / Vehicles
           4   5
   d. <u>Idaho</u> / Department / of /
        2   3
    Environmental / Quality
     Correct order <u>a, d, c, b</u>

4. a.   2   3
    <u>6th</u> / Avenue / Pizza
          2   3
   b. <u>Sixth</u> / Street / Secondhand
          2
   c. <u>600</u> / Flowers
          2   3
   d. <u>16</u> / Flags / Parks
     Correct order <u>a, d, c, b</u>

5. a.   2   4   5   3
    <u>Dexter</u> / County / Bureau / of / Licenses
       2 3   4   5
   b. City / of / <u>Dexter</u> / Municipal / Library
        2   3
   c. <u>Dexter</u> / City / Hall
          2   3   4
   d. <u>Dexter</u> / County / Circuit / Court
     Correct order <u>c, b, d, a</u>

6. a. Kypriaki Dimokratia (Greek) and Kibris
                        2   3
    Cumhuriyeti (Turkish), (Republic / of /
    <u>Cyprus</u>)
                           2   3
   b. République du Tchad, (Republic / of / <u>Chad</u>)
                         2   3
   c. República de Cabo Verde, (Republic / of /
    <u>Cape Verde</u>)
                      2   3
   d. Kampuchea, (Kingdom / of / <u>Cambodia</u>)
     Correct order <u>d, c, b, a</u>

2. Cross-references for No. 6

Original	Cross-Reference
a. Cyprus Republic of	Kypriaki Dimokratia
	SEE Cyprus Republic of
a. Cyprus Republic of	Kibris Cumhuriyeti
	SEE Cyprus Republic of
b. Chad Republic of	République du Tchad
	SEE Chad Republic of
c. Cape Verde Republic of	República de Cabo Verde
	SEE Cape Verde Republic of
d. Cambodia Kingdom of	Kampuchea
	SEE Cambodia Kingdom of

Activity 4-3   Coding and Arranging II

1. a.   ²   ³
    <u>Vantage</u> / Point / Spa
     ⁶   ⁷
    2d / Avenue
     ⁴   ⁵
    Raleigh, / North Carolina
       ²   ³
  b. <u>Van</u> / Delivery / Service
        ²   ³
  c. <u>Vantage</u> / Point / Spa
     ⁶   ⁷
    31st / Street
     ⁴   ⁵
    Erie, / Pennsylvania
     ⁴   ²   ³
  d. Mrs. / Melinda / R. / <u>Van Arsdale</u>
       ²   ³
  e. <u>Vantage</u> / Point / Spa
     ⁶   ⁷
    Eastern / Parkway
     ⁴   ⁵
    Blacksburg, / Virginia
    Correct order <u>b, d, e, c, a</u>

2. a.   ²
    <u>Country</u> / Kitchen
     ⁵   ⁶
    34th / Avenue
     ³   ⁴
    Newark, / New Jersey
       ²   ³   ⁴
  b. <u>22nd</u> / Street / Photo / Lab
         ²
  c. <u>Country</u> / Kitchen
     ⁵   ⁶
    18th / Street
     ³   ⁴
    Newark, / New Jersey

  d.   ²   ³   ⁴   ⁵
    <u>10</u> / Little / Indians / Day / Care
        ²
  e. <u>Country</u> / Kitchen
     ⁵   ⁶
    First / Avenue
     ³   ⁴
    Newark, / New Jersey
    Correct order <u>d, b, c, a, e</u>

3. a.   ⁴   ²   ³
    Admiral / Girard / T. / <u>Schulte</u>
               ²
  b. <u>Schueler-Dillworth</u> / Designs
        ²
  c. Muriel / <u>Schumacher</u>
        ²
  d. Heather / <u>Schuman-Lee</u>
     ⁴   ²   ³
  e. The / <u>Schuman</u> / Education / Center
    Correct order <u>b, a, c, e, d</u>

4. a.   ²   ³   ⁴
    <u>Eaton</u> / City / Water / Works
     ²   ³   ⁵   ⁶   ⁴
  b. City / of / <u>Etna</u> / Department / of / Health
       ²   ³
  c. <u>Pasadena</u> / Public / Library
      ²   ³   ⁴
  d. <u>Pinellas</u> / County / Historical / Society
      ²   ³
  e. <u>Eaton</u> / City / Hall
    Correct order <u>e, a, b, c, d</u>

2. Cross-references for No. 3

Original	**Cross-Reference**
b. SchuelerDillworth Designs	DillworthSchueler Designs
	SEE SchuelerDillworth Designs
d. SchumanLee Heather	Lee Heather Schuman
	SEE SchumanLee Heather

Activity 4-4   Mystery Sentence Puzzle

The sentence is *spell out symbols.*

Activity 4-5   Coding and Arranging County Names

Note: Students were instructed to begin numbering with Unit 3, as the first two units of each item are *Marion, County.*

__11__ 1. Administration / Services, / Motor / Pool, / Transportation / Department
　　　　5　　　　6　　7　　8　　　3　　　　4

__7__ 2. Aging / Agency, / Social / Services / Division, / Human / Services / Department
　　　9　　10　　6　　7　　8　　3　　4　　　5

__6__ 3. Well / Child / Clinics, / Public / Health / Division, / Human / Services / Department
　　　9　10　11　6　　7　　8　　3　　4　　5

__12__ 4. Operations / and / Administration, / Transportation / Department
　　　　5　　6　　　7　　　　3　　　　4

__9__ 5. Crime / Analysis, / Sheriff's / Department
　　　5　6　　3　　4

__8__ 6. Public / Library
　　　3　　4

__2__ 7. Marriage / Licenses, / Clerk's / Office
　　　5　　6　　3　　4

__1__ 8. Budget / Office, / Treasurer
　　　3　4　5

__13__ 9. Land / Use / Planning, / Planning / Services, / Transportation / Department
　　　7　8　9　　5　　6　　3　　4

__14__ 10. Service / District / No. / 1, / Utilities / Department
　　　5　6　7　8　3　4

__3__ 11. 911 / Coordinator, / General / Service / Department
　　　6　7　3　4　5

6   7   3   4   5

__5__ 12. Housing / Authority, / Human / Services / Department

5   3   4

__10__ 13. Traffic, / Sheriff's / Department

6   7   3   4   5

__4__ 14. Personnel / Office, / Human / Resources / Department

Activity 4-6   Coding and Arranging by Subject

Key Unit	Unit 2	Unit 3	Unit 4	Unit 5
Applications	Accounting	Clerk	Bernstein	Mike
Applications	Accounting	Clerk	Heider	Erika
Applications	Accounting	Clerk	Minten	Janelle
Applications	Accounting	Clerk	Norton	Linda
Applications	Accounting	Clerk	Ridgway	Anita
Applications	Accounting	Clerk	Ruiz	Florendo
Applications	Accounting	Clerk	Sheng	Cherie
Applications	Accounting	Clerk	Yukimura	Akeo
Applications	Records	Clerk	Burns	Gene
Applications	Records	Clerk	Clarke	Susan
Applications	Records	Clerk	Miller	Doreen
Applications	Records	Clerk	Nguyen	Thao
Applications	Records	Clerk	Smith	Mark
Applications	Records	Clerk	Woods	Clara
Applications	Records	Supervisor	DelGado	Beatriz
Applications	Records	Supervisor	Dodd	Lila
Applications	Records	Supervisor	Jones	Kelly
Applications	Records	Supervisor	McDowell	Samuel
Applications	Records	Supervisor	Moore	Verna
Applications	Records	Supervisor	Mostifavi	AlSeyed

ELECTRONIC FILE MANAGEMENT

Terms

Directions: Fill in the missing word(s) in the space provided at the left.

1. _____   1. A(n) _____ consists of all the fields related to one person or topic.

2. _____   2. An acronym for the American Standard Code for Information Interchange is _____.

3. _____   3. A(n) _____ is a copy of electronic files and/or folders made as a precaution against the loss or damage of the original data.

4. _____   4. A(n) _____ zero is added to the front of a number so that all numbers are the same number of digits and the computer will read the numbers in numeric order.

5. _____   5. A(n) _____ is a set of one or more characters treated as a unit of information and part of a record in a database.

6. _____   6. A subdivision created by the computer's operating system on a disk is called a(n) _____.

7. _____   7. A(n) _____ is an organized collection of software that controls the overall operations of the computer.

8. _____   8. A(n) _____ is a unique name given to a file stored for computer use that must follow the computer's operating system rules.

9. _____   9. A(n) _____ is a collection of related data organized for rapid search and retrieval using a computer.

10. _____   10. A database element containing a group of records related to one subject or topic is called a(n) _____.

11. _____   11. A notation that includes a drive designation and the folders that indicate the location of a computer file is called a(n) _____.

12. _____   12. A(n) _____ is a handheld computer that is portable, easy to use, and capable of sharing information with a desktop or notebook computer.

13. _____   13. A database object used to instruct the program to find specific
                                   information is called a(n) _____.

14. _____   14. ASCII is a(n) _____ that was developed as a standard and logical way to
                                   recognize data on computers.

15. _____   15. The process of bringing items into agreement is called _____.

True/False

Directions: Circle T if the statement is true; circle F if the statement is false.

T   F   1. An *Access* database will allow the same data to be entered in the primary key field for two or
            more records.

T   F   2. Word processing and spreadsheet computer applications can perform alphabetic sorts on lists
            of names.

T   F   3. The ASCII values are numeric values assigned to specific characters.

T   F   4. The fields in a database application compare to individual facts about an item or a person.

T   F   5. A database query helps a user find specific information.

T   F   6. Most records departments do not create a database index of their paper and/or non-paper records.

Multiple Choice

Directions: Circle the letter of the best answer.

1. Using ASCII values for all characters, the computer sorts
   a. from lowest to highest.
   b. numbers before alphabetic letters.
   c. capital letters before lowercase letters.
   d. all the above.

2. A field in a database may contain
   a. one fact about a person or an item.
   b. many facts about one person or item.
   c. all the collected facts about many items or people.
   d. an area marked with boundaries.

3. The life cycle of electronic records includes
   a. creation and storage, distribution and use, and disposition.
   b. creation and storage, distribution and use, and maintenance.
   c. creation and storage, distribution and use, maintenance, and disposition.
   d. distribution and use, maintenance, and disposition.

4. A personal digital assistant is
   a. a portable handheld computer that is easy to use and capable of sharing information with a desktop or notebook computer.
   b. a portable computer about the size of an 8½″ × 11″ piece of paper.
   c. an electronic calendar only.
   d. an address book and an electronic calendar only.

5. When saving and naming electronic files, make sure that
   a. the filenames are numbered consecutively.
   b. the filenames are meaningful to help you locate the files again.
   c. the filenames contain no more than seven characters.
   d. you place the files in a folder with today's date.

6. The process of bringing items into agreement (for example, updating the data on a PC and a PDA so that both contain the same data) is
   a. retrieval.
   b. resolution.
   c. synchronization.
   d. records transfer.

Activity 5-1   Determining Fields for a Member Database

Directions: As secretary of your school's Business Club, you have been asked to create a member database. The database should identify each member's ID number, name, address, phone number, e-mail address, favorite class, and career objective. In the following table, write the field names you will use and the information to be contained in each field.

Field Name	Field Contents

Activity 5-2   Organizing Your E-Mail

Directions: Your e-mail inbox has over 300 messages! Something must be done quickly to remedy the problem. Outline the steps you will take to organize your e-mail inbox.

1. _____

2. _____

3. _____

4. _____

Activity 5-3   Using Your PDA

Directions: You were just given a personal digital assistant. In the space provided, identify two or three features of your new PDA that most appeal to you. Also indicate what everyday tasks each feature will enable you to perform.

Feature	Tasks
1.	
2.	
3.	
4.	
5.	

Activity 5-4   Organizing Electronic Files

Directions: While working on your computer, you were unable to find a file needed to complete a homework assignment. You decide to organize your files by creating individual folders for each of the courses you are taking this semester. Below is a list of the files you have for your courses. In the space provided, write the name of the folder you would create; then write the names of the files you would place in the folder.

Multimedia.ppt for Computer Applications
Rembrandt.html for Art History
Spelling Demons.doc for Creative Writing
Classmates.mdb for Computer Applications
Customers.mdb for Records Management
Essay 1.doc for Creative Writing
Galina Enterprises.xls for Accounting I
Depreciation.xls for Computer Applications

Essay2.doc for Creative Writing
Broadband.mdb for Records Management
Newsletter.doc for Computer Applications
Da Vinci.html for Art History
Service Business.doc for Accounting I
Short Story.doc for Creative Writing
PDAs.html for Computer Applications

Folder Name	Filenames

SOLUTIONS

Terms

1. record
2. ASCII
3. backup
4. leading
5. field
6. directory (or folder)
7. operating system
8. filename
9. database
10. table
11. path
12. personal digital assistant (PDA)
13. query
14. character code
15. synchronization

True/False

1. F
2. T
3. T
4. T
5. T
6. F

Multiple Choice

1. d
2. a
3. c
4. a
5. b
6. c

Activity 5-1   Determining Fields for a Member Database

Answers will vary slightly but should include the following:

Field Name	Field Contents
ID	Member ID number
First Name	Member first name
Last Name	Member last name
Address	Member street address
City	Member city
State	Member state
ZIP	Member ZIP
Phone	Member's phone number
E-mail	Member's e-mail address
Fav Class	Member's favorite class
Career Obj	Member's career objective

Activity 5-2   Organizing Your E-Mail

Answers will vary but should include the following:
- Deleting files that are no longer needed
- Creating folders to organize e-mail by person or organization

Activity 5-3   Using Your PDA

Answers will vary depending on personal preferences. Some features that might be listed are as follows:
- Portability
- Ease of use
- Storage capability
- Perform calculations
- Ability to share information with a desktop or laptop computer
- Ability to connect to the Internet
- Ability to act as a global positioning system (GPS)

Activity 5-4   Organizing Electronic Files

Folder names will vary. A course number (Art History 102) may or may not be assigned, and filenames may or may not be alphabetized within each folder.

Folder Name	Filenames
Accounting I	Galina Enterprises.xls
	Service Business.doc
Art History	Da Vinci.html
	Rembrandt.html
Creative Writing	Essay 1.doc
	Essay 2.doc
	Short Story.doc
	Spelling Demons.doc
Computer Applications	Classmates.mdb
	Depreciation.xls
	Multimedia.ppt
	Newsletter.doc
	PDAs.html
Records Management	Broadband.mdb
	Customers.mdb

ALPHABETIC RECORDS MANAGEMENT, EQUIPMENT, AND PROCEDURES

Terms

Directions: Fill in the missing word(s) in the space provided at the left.

1. _____

2. _____

3. _____

4. _____

5. _____

6. _____

7. _____

8. _____

9. _____

10. _____

11. _____

12. _____

1. A device that contains the name of the subject or number given to the file folder contents is called a(n) _____.

2. A series of shelving units that move on tracks to allow access to files are called _____.

3. The consistent use of different colors for different supplies in a storage system is called _____.

4. _____ are rigid dividers with projecting tabs used in files to identify sections and to facilitate reference to a particular record location.

5. Containers used to hold stored records in an orderly manner are called _____.

6. The use of different colors to divide the alphabet sections in a storage system is called _____.

7. A folder that has a top flap and sides with creases along its bottom and sides that allow it to expand like an accordion is called a(n) _____.

8. A(n) _____ is a systematic way of storing records according to an alphabetic, subject, numeric, geographic, or chronologic arrangement.

9. Placing records into a folder in a file drawer (or on a shelf) or electronically saving a record is called _____.

10. Going directly to a file without referencing an index to find a record is called a(n) _____ method.

11. A(n) _____ folder has built-in hooks on each side that hang from rails on each side of a file drawer or other storage equipment.

12. A projection for a caption on a folder or guide that extends above the regular height or beyond the regular width of the folder or guide is a(n) _____.

13. _____

13. _____ are conventional storage cabinets that are deeper than they are wide and have files arranged from front to back.

14. _____

14. A(n) _____ is a device at the back of a file drawer that can be moved to allow contraction or expansion of the drawer contents.

15. _____

15. _____ is the first step in the storage procedures in which the record is checked for its readiness to be filed.

16. _____

16. Special folders that replace complete folders that have been removed from storage are _____.

17. _____

17. A(n) _____ is storage equipment that is wider than it is deep with records accessed from the side (horizontally).

18. _____

18. A control device that shows the location of borrowed records is a(n) _____.

19. _____

19. A form that is inserted in place of a record removed from a folder is a(n) _____.

20. _____

20. The location of the tab across the top or down the side of a guide or folder is the _____.

21. _____

21. An agreed-upon mark such as initials or a symbol placed on a record to show that the record is ready for storage is a(n) _____.

22. _____

22. A device used to arrange records into alphabetic or numeric categories and to hold records temporarily prior to storage is a(n) _____.

23. _____

23. A divider used to lead the eye quickly to a specific place in the file is a(n) _____.

24. _____

24. Steps for the orderly arrangement of records as required by a specific storage method or records management system are known as _____.

25. _____

25. Arranging records in proper sequence to facilitate storage is _____.

26. _____

26. _____ contain records to and from correspondents with a small volume of records that does not require an individual folder.

27. _____

27. _____ contain records of correspondents with enough records to warrant separate folders.

28. _____

28. A(n) _____ is a divider that identifies a main division of a file.

29. _____

29. A date-sequenced file by which matters pending are flagged for attention on the proper date is called a(n) _____.

30. _____

30. Words on a label that identify the contents of a drawer, shelf, or folder are called a(n) _____.

True/False

Directions: Circle T if the statement is true; circle F if the statement is false.

T F 1. The number of paper documents is decreasing rapidly, and businesses will not need manual filing equipment and supplies five years from now.

T F 2. In an alphabetic correspondence file, an individual folder is prepared for each correspondent.

T F 3. Traditional vertical file cabinets are available in the four-drawer size only.

T F 4. A primary guide is a divider that identifies a main division of a file and precedes all other material in a section.

T F 5. When choosing storage equipment, the type and volume of records to be stored and retrieved is one consideration.

Multiple Choice

Directions: Circle the letter of the best answer.

1. Which of the following statements is NOT an advantage of the alphabetic storage method?
   a. The alphabetic storage method is a direct access method.
   b. A-to-Z order of records is simple to understand.
   c. Names on folders are seen by anyone who happens to glance at an open storage container.
   d. Cost of operation may be lower than other methods.

2. Which of the following shows the correct order of the storage procedures?
   a. Inspecting, indexing, cross-referencing, coding, sorting, and storing.
   b. Indexing, coding, inspecting, sorting, cross-referencing, and storing.
   c. Indexing, sorting, inspecting, cross-referencing, coding, and storing.
   d. Inspecting, indexing, coding, cross-referencing, sorting, and storing.

3. Placing a guide or sheet in a location that is frequently assumed to be the location of a record or folder is
   a. indexing.
   b. coding.
   c. cross-referencing.
   d. inspecting.

4. On incoming business correspondence in an alphabetic records system, the name for storage purposes is usually
   a. the name signed in the signature block.
   b. in the letter address.
   c. in the letterhead.
   d. none of the above.

5. Marking the units of the filing segment on a record is called
   a. indexing.
   b. coding.
   c. cross-referencing.
   d. inspecting.

Activity 6-1   Identify the Parts of a File Arrangement

Directions: Identify parts A, B, C, D, and E in the following illustration by writing the correct term in the appropriate blank following the illustration.

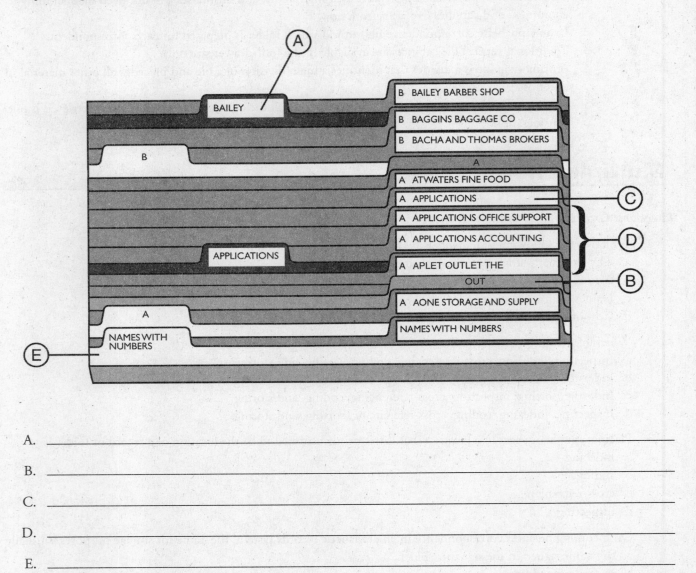

A. _____

B. _____

C. _____

D. _____

E. _____

Activity 6-2   Correct Sequence for Storage Procedures

1. Directions: *Write the correct order for performing the storage procedures by numbering 1–6 in the space before the description.*

_____ a. Physically mark the filing segment.

_____ b. Check to see that the record is ready to be stored.

_____ c. Arrange the records in sequence to facilitate storage.

_____ d. Mentally determine the filing segment.

_____ e. Place the record into the proper storage container.

_____ f. Prepare any aids to help in finding the record if the record is requested by a name other than the filing segment.

2. Directions: *Write the name of the storage procedure described in No. 1 above in the space provided.*

a. _____

b. _____

c. _____

d. _____

e. _____

f. _____

Activity 6-3 Storage Equipment and Floor Space

Directions:

1. *Calculate the number and type of storage units for the following scenarios. Write your answers in the designated space below the scenario and show your calculations. Assume that 3 linear inches will be left in each drawer or on each shelf to allow space for storing and retrieving records and that file cabinets or shelves are of the dimensions illustrated in Chapter 6 of the textbook. Round answers to the next whole number (regardless of the fractional part). Write a sentence explaining your choice of equipment for each scenario.*

   ### Scenario A
   A medical clinic has a patient correspondent file in an area with open access to people other than filers. There is a limited amount of aisle space for the storage cabinets. Currently there are 1,857 linear inches of records including guides and folders.

   Equipment Type _____   Total # Drawers or Shelves _____

   No. of Units Required _____

   Explanation _____

   ### Scenario B
   A large legal office keeps its client records in a security vault. The firm currently has 2,178 linear feet of records including guides and folders. At times, three to five people may be accessing the files.

   Equipment Type _____   Total # Drawers or Shelves _____

   No. of Units Required _____

   Explanation _____

2. *For each scenario, calculate the amount of total floor space required by the equipment selected. Include drawer-pull space but not aisle space. Round your answer to the nearest square foot.*

   Scenario A _____

   Scenario B _____

SOLUTIONS

Terms

1. label
2. mobile shelving
3. color accenting
4. guides
5. folders
6. color coding
7. bellows (expansion) folder
8. storage (filing) method
9. storage
10. direct access
11. suspension (hanging)
12. tab
13. vertical file cabinets
14. follower block (compressor)
15. inspecting
16. OUT folders
17. lateral file cabinet
18. OUT indicator
19. OUT sheet
20. position
21. release mark
22. sorter
23. special (auxiliary) guide
24. storage procedures
25. sorting
26. general folders
27. individual folders
28. primary guide
29. tickler file
30. caption

True/False

1. F
2. F
3. F
4. T
5. T

Multiple Choice

1. c
2. d
3. c
4. c
5. b

Activity 6-1   Identify the Parts of a File Arrangement

A. special guide
B. OUT indicator (guide or folder)
C. general folder
D. special folders
E. primary guide

Activity 6-2   Correct Sequence for Storage Procedures

1. Correct order

	2. Name of procedure
__3__ a.	a. coding
__1__ b.	b. inspecting
__5__ c.	c. sorting
__2__ d.	d. indexing
__6__ e.	e. storing
__4__ f.	f. cross-referencing

Activity 6-3   Storage Equipment and Floor Space

1. Answers for Scenarios A and B appear below.

    Scenario A
    Equipment Type: lateral files   Total # Drawers or Shelves: 57
    No. of Units Required: 15 for 4-drawer cabinets and 19 for 3-drawer cabinets
    1,857 linear inches divided by 33 per drawer = 56.2 = 57 total drawers required
    57 divided by 4 = 14.3 = 15 file cabinets (4-drawer)
    57 divided by 3 = 19 file cabinets (3-drawer)

    Explanation: Open-shelf files allow people in the file area to see patient names. The next type of storage requiring less space is lateral file cabinets, which keep records confidential and can be locked.

    Scenario B
    Equipment Type: shelf files   Total # Drawers or Shelves: 792
    No. of Units Required: 114 for 3-foot-wide shelf units
    2,178 linear ft. × 12 in. per ft. = 26,136 linear inches
    26,136 divided by 33 = 791.9 = 792 total shelves required
    792 divided by 7 shelves per unit = 113.1 = 114 shelf units

    Explanation: The volume of records and the number of people accessing files indicate shelf files; the vault protects the confidentiality and security of the open-shelf files.

2. Answers for Scenarios A and B appear below.

    Scenario A
    83 sq. ft. or 105 sq. ft. (15 × 5.5 = 82.5 sq. ft. or 19 × 5.5 = 104.5 sq. ft.)

    Scenario B
    342 sq. ft. (114 × 3 sq. ft. = 342 sq. ft.)

STORING, RETRIEVING, AND TRANSFERRING RECORDS

Terms

Directions: Fill in the missing word(s) in the space provided at the left.

1. _____

2. _____

3. _____

4. _____

5. _____

6. _____

7. _____

8. _____

9. _____

10. _____

11. _____

12. _____

1. A record needed to perform current operations is called a(n) _____.

2. A control procedure to establish the current location of a record when it is not in the records center or central file is called _____.

3. A significant, vital, or important record of continuing value to be protected, managed, and retained is called a(n) _____.

4. A record that does not have to be readily available but must be kept for legal, fiscal, or historical purposes is called a(n) _____.

5. A notification of the scheduled destruction of records is a(n) _____.

6. The official copy of a record that is retained for legal, operational, or historical purposes is called the _____.

7. A method of transferring active records at the end of a stated period, usually one year, to inactive storage is called the _____ transfer method.

8. A(n) _____ record has continuing or historical value and is preserved permanently.

9. Locating and removing a record from a filing system or records center is called _____.

10. A written request for a record or for information from a record is called a(n) _____.

11. An office designated to maintain the record or official copy of a particular record is the _____.

12. A detailed listing that could include the types, locations, dates, volumes, equipment, classification systems, and usage data of records is called a(n) _____.

13. _____

13. The method used to transfer records continuously from active to inactive storage areas whenever they are no longer needed is _____.

14. _____

14. A system for ensuring the timely and proper return of materials charged out from a file is known as _____.

15. _____

15. A(n) _____ is a list containing specific records needed for a given program or project.

16. _____

16. A(n) _____ is a form for recording what record was taken; when it was taken; who took it; the due date; the return date; the date an overdue notice was sent; and, if necessary, an extended due date.

17. _____

17. _____ is the act of relocating records from one storage area to another.

18. _____

18. A group of related records filed and used as a unit and evaluated as a unit for retention purposes is called a(n) _____.

19. _____

19. After records have reached the end of their retention period in active and/or inactive storage, they may be transferred to an archives for retention or be destroyed. This phase of the records life cycle is called _____.

20. _____

20. A(n) _____ is a tickler file containing copies of forms completed when records are received in a records center.

21. _____

21. A(n) _____ is a list of records series titles, indicating for each series the length of time it is to be maintained.

22. _____

22. _____ is the disposal of records of no further value by various means.

23. _____

23. A(n) _____ is a low-cost centralized area for housing and servicing inactive records whose reference rate does not warrant their retention in the prime office space.

24. _____

24. A(n) _____ file is a tickler file that contains the requisition forms filed by dates that records are due back in the inactive records center.

25. _____

25. A(n) _____ is an item that is not usually included within the scope of official records, such as a convenience file, a day file, reference materials, and drafts, and is not required to be retained.

True/False

Directions: Circle T if the statement is true; circle F if the statement is false.

T   F   1. A hold can be placed on records scheduled for destruction.

T   F   2. All records kept in an office are official records.

T   F   3. If someone borrows a nonrecord, a charge-out procedure needs to be followed.

T   F   4. Transferring records to inactive storage is part of the disposition phase of the records life cycle.

T   F   5. Correspondence records should be transferred using the periodic transfer method.

Multiple Choice

Directions: Circle the letter of the best answer.

1. A student graduated from college two years ago. In the registrar's office at the college, the student's transcript is now classified as
   a. active.
   b. not yet filed.
   c. inactive.
   d. archive.

2. Records center boxes need to be
   a. purchased from the same supplier.
   b. a distinctive color.
   c. waterproof.
   d. of uniform size.

3. Records transfer involves moving records to one of three destinations: destruction, permanent retention, or
   a. archive storage.
   b. inactive storage.
   c. active storage.
   d. permanent storage.

4. Usually charge-out procedures consist of
   a. using OUT indicators only.
   b. using OUT indicators and disposing of OUT indicators after a record has been returned.
   c. disposing of OUT indicators after materials have been returned.
   d. using OUT indicators, carrier folders, and a charge-out log.

5. One classification of records to determine how long to retain them is by value to the organization. The categories are
   a. useless, useful, important, and legal.
   b. unimportant, important, vital, and essential.
   c. nonessential, useless, vital, and essential.
   d. nonessential, useful, important, and vital.

Activity 7-1   Requisition, Charge-Out, and Follow-Up Procedures

You are an administrative assistant for the Brinkman & Logan Law Firm. Among your duties, you are responsible for the records in your department, Corporate Law. The usual check-out time period is one week.

1. *Directions: Complete records requisition forms for the following requests for records made during the week of April 26 to April 30.*

   April 26: Tom Brinkman, Corporate Law, X3645, called to request a letter dated 4/15 from Paul Richards about the Georgia-Atlantic siding case.

   April 27: Latisha Kennedy, Administrative Services, e-mail: lkennedy@bllf.com, requested the letter dated 4/12 from Tran Nguyen about his will.

   April 28: Frank Smith, Human Resources, X3425, requested Jacqueline Howard's application letter dated March 30.

   April 29: Tom Brinkman returned the Georgia-Atlantic letter of 4/15.

   April 30: Frank Smith returned Jacqueline Howard's application letter.

Records Request	
Name on Record	Date on Record
Date Borrowed	Date to Be Returned
Requester Name	Extension
Department	E-mail
Place white copy into folder. Place blue copy into tickler control file.	
Form 209 (Rev. 07/09)	

Records Request	
Name on Record	Date on Record
Date Borrowed	Date to Be Returned
Requester Name	Extension
Department	E-mail
Place white copy into folder. Place blue copy into tickler control file.	
Form 209 (Rev. 07/09)	

Records Request	
Name on Record	Date on Record
Date Borrowed	Date to Be Returned
Requester Name	Extension
Department	E-mail
Place white copy into folder. Place blue copy into tickler control file.	
Form 209 (Rev. 07/09)	

2. Directions: Complete the following charge-out log using the information from No. 1.

	Charge-Out Log							
Name on Record	Date on Record	Name of Person Borrowing Record	Ext. or E-mail	Date Borrowed	Date Due	Date Returned	Date Overdue Notice Sent	Ext. Due Date
Form 211 (Revised 07/09)								

3. Directions: Complete the charge-out log for the follow-up step. Today's date is May 6. On the line below, list the name of anyone who would receive an overdue notice.

_____

Activity 7-2   Retrieving Information

Directions: Use some type of computer database, such as an encyclopedic CD on a computer, a website, an online catalog at your library, or any other good source, to find information about the following topics. Write your answers on the lines provided.

1. What is the National Archives and Records Administration (NARA)?

     _____

     _____

     _____

     _____

2. What is the name of another archives—public or private? What type(s) of documents or records are stored in the archives?

     _____

     _____

     _____

     _____

3. What are some other uses of RFID technology in addition to inventorying records and charging in/out records?

     _____

     _____

     _____

     _____

Activity 7-3   Applying a Records Retention Schedule

Directions: Refer to the records retention schedule shown in Figure 7.3 in the textbook to determine the destruction date of the following records.

Type of Record	Dates on Records	Destruction Dates
1. Claims, group life	January 1–June 30, 2009	
2. Accounts payable invoices	January 1–December 31, 2008	
3. Records destruction documentation	July 1–December 31, 2004	
4. Office equipment records	September 1–December 31, 2006	
5. Employment terminations	January 1–December 31, 2009	
6. Bank statements	January 1–December 31, 2007	
7. Advertising artwork	December 31, 2002	
8. Employee vacation records	January 1–December 31, 2004	
9. Accounts receivable ledger	April 1–June 30, 2005	
10. Records inventory	July 1, 2009	

SOLUTIONS

Terms

1. active record
2. charge-out
3. official record
4. inactive record
5. destruction notice
6. record copy
7. periodic
8. archive
9. retrieval
10. requisition
11. office of record
12. records inventory
13. perpetual transfer
14. follow-up
15. pick list
16. charge-out log
17. records transfer
18. records series
19. records disposition
20. destruction date file
21. records retention schedule
22. records destruction
23. records center
24. charge-out and follow-up
25. nonrecord

True/False

1. T
2. F
3. F
4. T
5. T

Multiple Choice

1. c
2. d
3. b
4. d
5. d

Activity 7-1 Requisition, Charge-Out, and Follow-Up Procedures

1. Requisition Forms

Records Request	
Name on Record *Georgia-Atlantic*	Date on Record *4/15*
Date Borrowed *4/26*	Date to Be Returned *5/3*
Requester Name *Tom Brinkman*	Extension *3645*
Department *Corporate Law*	E-mail
Place white copy into folder. Place blue copy into tickler control file.	
Form 209 (Rev. 07/09)	

Records Request	
Name on Record *Nguyen, Tran*	Date on Record *4/12*
Date Borrowed *4/27*	Date to Be Returned *5/4*
Requester Name *Latisha Kennedy*	Extension
Department *Administrative Services*	E-mail *lkennedy@bllf.com*
Place white copy into folder. Place blue copy into tickler control file.	
Form 209 (Rev. 07/09)	

Records Request	
Name on Record *Applications—Howard, Jacqueline*	Date on Record *3/30*
Date Borrowed *4/28*	Date to Be Returned *5/5*
Requester Name *Frank Smith*	Extension *3425*
Department *Human Resources*	E-mail
Place white copy into folder. Place blue copy into tickler control file.	
Form 209 (Rev. 07/09)	

2. Charge-Out Log

Charge-Out Log								
Name on Record	Date on Record	Name of Person Borrowing Record	Ext. or E-mail	Date Borrowed	Date Due	Date Returned	Date Overdue Notice Sent	Ext. Due Date
Georgia-Atlantic	4/15	Tom Brinkman	3645	4/26	5/3	4/29		
Nguyen, Tran	4/12	Latisha Kennedy	lkennedy@bllf.com	4/27	5/4		5/6	
Applications Jacqueline Howard	3/30	Frank Smith	3425	4/28	5/5	4/30		

3. Latisha Kennedy would receive an overdue notice.

Activity 7-2   Retrieving Information

Possible answers

1. The National Archives and Records Administration (NARA) is an independent federal agency that helps preserve U.S. history by overseeing the management of all federal records. NARA is directed by the Archivist of the United States.

2. Responses will vary. Possible examples include an archives at a large university or a well-known movie or photo archives.

3. Responses will vary. One response may be that retailers will soon require RFID tags on boxes and skids of merchandise shipped from all vendors.

Activity 7-3   Applying a Records Retention Schedule

Type of Record	Dates on Records	Destruction Dates
1. Claims, group life	January 1–June 30, 2009	July 1, 2013
2. Accounts payable invoices	January 1–December 31, 2008	January 1, 2015
3. Records destruction documentation	July 1–December 31, 2004	Do not destroy
4. Office equipment records	September 1–December 31, 2006	January 1, 2013
5. Employment terminations	January 1–December 31, 2009	January 1, 2011
6. Bank statements	January 1–December 31, 2007	January 1, 2014
7. Advertising artwork	December 31, 2002	Do not destroy
8. Employee vacation records	January 1–December 31, 2004	January 1, 2012
9. Accounts receivable ledger	April 1–June 30, 2005	July 1, 2011
10. Records inventory	July 1, 2009	July 2, 2010

NAME: _____

SUBJECT RECORDS MANAGEMENT

Terms

Directions: Fill in the missing word(s) in the space provided at the left.

1. _____
2. _____
3. _____
4. _____
5. _____
6. _____
7. _____
8. _____
9. _____
10. _____

1. A listing of subject titles with numbers assigned is a(n) _____.

2. Storing and retrieving records by subject or topic is known as _____.

3. A subject filing arrangement in which the main subjects are arranged in alphabetic order with their subdivisions also arranged alphabetically is the _____ arrangement.

4. A method of access to records requiring prior use of an index is called _____.

5. The procedure of filing a record under an alternative subject topic to refer the file user to the original subject location of the record is called _____.

6. In the _____ arrangement, subject folders are arranged behind A-to-Z primary guides in their correct alphabetic order by subject title.

7. A printed alphabetic list of all subjects used as subject titles for records storage is called a(n) _____.

8. If a specific name in a file can be found without first referring to an index, the file is _____.

9. The storage procedure of writing the filing segment on a document for subject records storage is called _____.

10. The _____ records management system is expensive because setting up the file requires an experienced file analyst and maintaining the file requires experienced filers.

True/False

Directions: Circle T if the statement is true; circle F if the statement is false.

T   F   1. The encyclopedic arrangement of files is most appropriate for files with a high volume of records that require subjects and subdivisions.

T   F   2. The master index includes all subject titles for all records stored, as well as synonymous related titles that might be used to store and retrieve records.

T   F   3. An advantage of subject records storage is that related records are kept together.

T   F   4. General subject folders are not used in subject records storage because each record is filed in a folder with a specific filename.

T   F   5. If correspondence is filed in a subject arrangement, a name index is required.

Multiple Choice

Directions: Circle the letter of the best answer.

1. A characteristic of subject records management is that
   a. labels on guides and folders are the same for all subject files.
   b. color coding is not used.
   c. all file users can remember the specific subject title for each record.
   d. it is an indirect access system.

2. An index listing of subject records by their file number is a
   a. master index.
   b. relative index.
   c. name index.
   d. numeric index.

3. When a record contains information on more than one subject, the file user will
   a. use another storage method.
   b. select the most important subject and cross-reference the other subject titles.
   c. use the subject title with the fewest records in the system.
   d. use the first subject title in the master index.

4. Which of the following statements best describes subject records storage?
   a. Cross-references are not necessary in the subject method.
   b. The master index should always be consulted to be sure the correct subject title is used.
   c. Records do not have to be released before storing in the subject method.
   d. Both a and c.

5. Indexing a record for subject storage means
   a. preparing a records index.
   b. writing or marking the subject title on the record.
   c. filing a copy under an alternative subject title.
   d. completing the mental process of deciding the filing segment.

Activity 8-1   Master Index

Directions: Prepare a master index for your personal records or for a subject file to which you have access. Use the space provided below.

Activity 8-2   Relative Index

Directions: Prepare a relative index from the following master index for the records management system of a high school. Add other titles by which you think records might be requested.

Master Index—Subject Files for Abbott Central High School	
Building and Grounds	Financial Records
Curriculum	Budget
Committees	Purchases
Course Syllabi	Salaries
Curriculum Guides	Travel and Expense
Departments	Vendors
Athletics	Human Resources
Electives	Biographical Data
Fine Arts	Certification Records
Language Arts	Professional Development
Mathematics	Policies and Procedures
Science	Board Policies
Social Studies	Handbooks
Technology	Statutes and Regulations
Equipment and Supplies	Projects
Catalogs	Reports
Furniture	Student Records
Inventories	Attendance
Laboratory	Contact Information
Media	Follow-Up Records
	Grades and Transcripts

Activity 8-3   Name Index

Directions:

1. Create a new database file named *SG Activity 8-3*.

2. Create a table named **Name Index** with the following fields: ID, Correspondent, Primary Subject, Subdivision, Address, City, State, ZIP. Select **AutoNumber** as the field type for the ID field. Select **Text** as the field type for all other fields. Select the **ID** field as the primary key.

3. Enter the data below into the Name Index table.

4. You have been asked to print a name index that can be used for reference in finding files requested by correspondent name. Create a report based on the Name Index table. Include all the fields in the report. Sort the data by the **Correspondent** field. Select the **Columnar** layout. Save the report as **Name Index Report.** Print the report.

5. You have been asked to provide a list of all correspondents filed under the primary subject *Construction*. Create a query based on the Name Index table. The query results should display the Subdivision, Correspondent, Address, City, State, and ZIP fields for records that have **Construction** in the Primary Subject field. Sort in ascending order on the **Correspondent** field. Save the query as **Construction Correspondents.** Print the query results.

M & R Drainage Systems
117542 Western Blvd.
Seattle, WA 98101-2345
Primary Subject: Construction
Subdivision: Plumbing

Lang Architectural Group, Inc.
3393 Downsfield Rd.
Pittsburgh, PA 15201-2373
Primary Subject: Architecture
Subdivision: Residential Designs

Custom Walls, Inc.
3805 Edwards Rd.
Honolulu, HI 96803-1454
Primary Subject: Construction
Subdivision: Drywall

Forrest Roofing
4509 Blossom Ave.
Atlanta, GA 30301-6743
Primary Subject: Construction
Subdivision: Roofing

Speck & Roberts Architects
15 S Main St.
Toledo, OH 43601-1544
Primary Subject: Architecture
Subdivision: Residential Designs

Alveraz Architects
34 Vine St.
Cincinnati, OH 45215-3852
Primary Subject: Architecture
Subdivision: Residential Designs

SOLUTIONS

Terms

1. number index
2. subject records management, subject filing, or subject records storage
3. encyclopedic
4. indirect access
5. cross-referencing
6. dictionary
7. master index, master list, subject index, or subject list
8. direct access
9. coding
10. subject

True/False

1. T
2. F
3. T
4. F
5. T

Multiple Choice

1. d
2. d
3. b
4. b
5. d

Activity 8-1   Master Index

Answers will vary, but students should show an encyclopedic arrangement of primary subjects with appropriate subdivisions.

Activity 8-2   Relative Index

Solutions will vary in format and content. However, all titles in the master index should be shown with additional appropriate subject titles. Each subject listing refers to the record location(s) for the topic. In this solution, possible additional titles are shown in bold italic print.

Relative Index—Subject Files for Abbott Central High School

Subject	Filed Under
Accounting	Financial Records
Applications	Human Resources
Athletics	Departments
Attendance	Student Records
Attendance Policy	Policies and Procedures
Biographical Data	Human Resources
Board Policies	Policies and Procedures
Budget	Financial Records
Buildings and Grounds	Building and Grounds
Career and Technical	Departments
Catalogs	Equipment and Supplies
Certification Records	Human Resources
Clubs and Organizations	Student Records
Committees	Curriculum
Contact Information	Student Records
Course Syllabi	Curriculum
Curriculum	Curriculum
Curriculum Guides	Curriculum
Departments	Departments
Electives	Departments
Equipment Maintenance	Equipment and Supplies
Equipment and Supplies	Equipment and Supplies
Faculty Handbook	Policies and Procedures
Fees	Financial Records
Financial Records	Financial Records
Fine Arts	Departments
Follow-Up Records	Student Records
Furniture	Equipment and Supplies
Grades and Transcripts	Student Records
Handbooks	Policies and Procedures
Inventories	Equipment and Supplies
Laboratory	Equipment and Supplies
Landscaping	Building and Grounds
Language Arts	Departments
Mathematics	Departments
Media	Equipment and Supplies
Parent and Community Projects	Projects
Human Resources	Human Resources
Policies and Procedures	Policies and Procedures
Professional Development	Human Resources
Projects	Projects
Purchases	Financial Records
Reports	Reports
Salaries	Financial Records
Science	Departments
Social Studies	Departments
Statutes and Regulations	Policies and Procedures
Student Handbook	Policies and Procedures
Student Records	Student Records
Technology	Departments
Travel and Expense	Financial Records
Vendors	Financial Records

Activity 8-3   Name Index

Name Index Report

Name Index Report

Correspondent	Alveraz Architects
ID	6
Primary Subject	Architecture
Subdivision	Residential Designs
Address	34 Vine St.
City	Cincinnati
State	OH
ZIP	45215-3852
Correspondent	Custom Walls, Inc.
ID	3
Primary Subject	Construction
Subdivision	Drywall
Address	3805 Edwards Rd.
City	Honolulu
State	HI
ZIP	96803-1454
Correspondent	Forrest Roofing
ID	4
Primary Subject	Construction
Subdivision	Roofing
Address	4509 Blossom Ave.
City	Atlanta
State	GA
ZIP	30301-6743

Correspondent	Lang Architectural Group, Inc.
ID	2
Primary Subject	Architecture
Subdivision	Residential Designs
Address	3393 Downsfield Rd.
City	Pittsburgh
State	PA
ZIP	15201-2373
Correspondent	M & R Drainage Systems
ID	1
Primary Subject	Construction
Subdivision	Plumbing
Address	117542 Western Blvd.
City	Seattle
State	WA
ZIP	98101-2345
Correspondent	Speck & Roberts Architects
ID	5
Primary Subject	Architecture
Subdivision	Residential Designs
Address	15 S Main St.
City	Toledo
State	OH
ZIP	43601-1544

Construction Correspondents Query

Construction Correspondents					
Subdivision	Correspondent	Address	City	State	ZIP
Drywall	Custom Walls, Inc.	3805 Edwards Rd.	Honolulu	HI	96803-1454
Roofing	Forrest Roofing	4509 Blossom Ave.	Atlanta	GA	30301-6743
Plumbing	M & R Drainage Systems	117542 Western Blvd.	Seattle	WA	98101-2345

NUMERIC RECORDS MANAGEMENT

Terms

Directions: Fill in the missing word(s) in the space provided at the left.

1. _____

2. _____

3. _____

4. _____

5. _____

6. _____

7. _____

8. _____

9. _____

10. _____

11. _____

12. _____

1. A numeric storage method in which the middle two or three digits of each number are used as the primary division under which a record is filed is _____ storage.

2. A systematic arrangement of records based on numbers is _____.

3. _____ is a numbering system that has blocks of numbers omitted and arranges records in a sequential order that differs from the consecutive order of numbers normally read from left to right.

4. The _____ is a serial list of numbers assigned to records in a numeric storage system.

5. A coding system that combines alphabetic and numeric characters is called _____ coding.

6. A coding system using numbers with two or more parts separated by a dash, space, or comma is known as _____ coding.

7. A(n) _____ is a list of correspondent names or subjects used in a numeric file with the assigned file codes indicated.

8. The _____ method is a method of numbering records in the order received and arranging them from lowest to highest numbers.

9. A numeric storage method in which the last two or three digits of each number are used as the primary division under which to file a record is _____ storage.

10. _____ is a system for coding records numerically in units of ten.

11. _____ is a coding system based on the assignment of groups of numbers to represent primary and secondary subjects.

12. _____ storage is a method of filing records by calendar date.

True/False

Directions: Circle T if the statement is true; circle F if the statement is false.

T F   1. Two storage methods—alphabetic and numeric—are involved in consecutive numeric records storage.

T F   2. Numeric storage is too complex for storing electronic records media.

T F   3. Numeric records storage is a direct access storage method.

T F   4. Alphabetic guides and folders are sometimes needed in numeric records storage.

T F   5. Cross-references are filed in the numeric file with related documents.

Multiple Choice

Directions: Circle the letter of the best answer.

1. Which of the following items is/are *not* used in the consecutive numbering method of records storage?
    a. Alphabetic guides and folders
    b. Accession log
    c. Master and relative indexes
    d. Numbered guides and folders

2. A disadvantage of the consecutive numbering method is that
    a. cross-references congest the files.
    b. expansion is difficult.
    c. congestion may occur at the end of the storage area.
    d. all the above.

3. An alphabetic index contains
    a. a correspondent's name.
    b. a date.
    c. a file code number.
    d. both a and c.

4. In numeric storage, a cross-reference is filed
    a. in the alphabetic index.
    b. in the accession log.
    c. in the numbered file.
    d. both a and b.

5. An advantage of using the terminal-digit storage method is that
    a. conversion is easier from a consecutively numbered arrangement to a terminal-digit arrangement than it is from a consecutively numbered arrangement to a middle-digit arrangement.
    b. people like to work with the method because it is easy to understand.
    c. several persons can store and retrieve consecutively numbered folders at the same time with no congestion at the workplace.
    d. training to use this method does not take as long as with other methods.

6. In numeric records storage, a database can be used to
    a. prepare and maintain the alphabetic index.
    b. prepare and maintain both the alphabetic index and the accession log.
    c. sort records before they are stored.
    d. all the above.

7. Which of the following are characteristics of alphanumeric coding?
    a. Letters and numbers are combined with punctuation marks.
    b. Main subjects are arranged alphabetically; their subdivisions are assigned a number.
    c. Main subjects are assigned numbers in groups to allow for expansion.
    d. All of the above.

8. The primary purpose of using an accession log is to
    a. have an alphabetic list of correspondents.
    b. create a numeric file list.
    c. provide information for a numeric records database.
    d. avoid assigning the same number twice.

Activity 9-1   Creating an Alphabetic Index

Directions: You have been asked to create a new database, enter data, and create a query.

1. Create a new *Access* file named *SG Activity 9-1.*

2. Create a new table named **Names and Subjects.** Include the following fields in the table: Record #, Code 1, Code 2, Code 3, Name or Subject. Make Record # a number field. Make all other fields text fields.

3. Enter data into the database table for the ten records shown on the following page. (You may want to create a form to make entering the data easier.) The numeric code is a three-part number and is to be entered into the three fields for code numbers. This arrangement allows correct sorting for different numbering systems. In the Name or Subject field, key the names and subjects with no punctuation in indexing order according to the alphabetic indexing rules. (Do not enter the addresses.)

4. Create a query named **Alphabetic Index** that displays these fields: Record #, Name or Subject, Code 1, Code 2, and Code 3. Design the query to sort the data by the Name or Subject field in ascending order. Check your work by viewing the list as a datasheet.

5. Print the query results.

Data for Activity 9-1 Alphabetic Index

Record No.	Name or Subject	Number Code
1	Maintenance Records	824 61 375
2	Mrs. Caroline Burrows 2330 Main St. Sun Valley, ID 83353-4728	711 40 298
3	Ms. Anu S. Johnson 127 S. Hill St. Stephen, MN 56757-2412	901 22 101
4	Hillcrest Tower Apartments 29890 Columbia Dr. Arcadia, SC 29320-8166	277 04 332
5	Woodland High School 4095 Melrose Blvd. Tulia, TX 79088-3211	424 92 719
6	Mr. Arden VanOettingen 14 Scarboro Ln. Ventura, IA 50482-4011	371 55 210
7	Sams Video Rentals 1166 Woton Dr. Wayne, NE 68787-6224	810 33 274
8	Charla Vaidyanathan, MD 1452 Kennebunk St. Monroe, CT 06468-3812	591 28 274
9	Southwest Designs 424 Waverly Pl. Liberal, KS 67901-7011	401 88 391
10	Office Supplies	133 71 390

Activity 9-2   Sorting for Consecutive Numeric Storage

Directions: You have been asked to design and print a query.

1. Open the *Access* file *SG Activity 9-1* that you created earlier.

2. Create a query named **Consecutive Sort** that displays these fields: Record #, Name or Subject, Code 1, Code 2, and Code 3. Design the query to sort the record number codes for consecutive numbering in ascending order.

3. Open the Datasheet view of the query and use it to indicate the order of the records by writing the record numbers (1–10) in the spaces provided below.

1. _____   6. _____

2. _____   7. _____

3. _____   8. _____

4. _____   9. _____

5. _____   10. _____

Activity 9-3   Sorting for Terminal-Digit Storage

Directions: You have been asked to design and print a query.

1. Open the *Access* file *SG Activity 9-1* that you updated earlier.

2. Create a query named **Terminal-Digit Sort** that displays these fields: Record #, Name or Subject, Code 1, Code 2, and Code 3. Design the query to sort the record number codes for terminal-digit numbering in ascending order. (Change the sort order of the numeric code columns.)

3. Open the Datasheet view of the query and use it to indicate the order of the records by writing the record numbers (1–10) in the spaces provided below.

1. _____   6. _____

2. _____   7. _____

3. _____   8. _____

4. _____   9. _____

5. _____   10. _____

Activity 9-4   Sorting for Middle-Digit Storage

Directions: You have been asked to design and print a query.

1. Open the *Access* file *SG Activity 9-1* that you updated earlier.

2. Create a query named **Middle-Digit Sort** that displays these fields: Record #, Name or Subject, Code 1, Code 2, and Code 3. Design the query to sort the record number codes for middle-digit numbering in ascending order. (Change the sort order of the numeric code columns.)

3. Open the Datasheet view of the query and use it to indicate the order of the records by writing the record numbers (1–10) in the spaces provided below.

1. _____   6. _____

2. _____   7. _____

3. _____   8. _____

4. _____   9. _____

5. _____   10. _____

SOLUTIONS

Terms

1. middle-digit
2. numeric records management
3. nonconsecutive numbering
4. accession log
5. alphanumeric
6. duplex-numeric
7. alphabetic index
8. consecutive numbering, serial numeric, sequential numeric, or straight numeric
9. terminal-digit
10. decimal-numeric
11. block-numeric
12. chronologic

True/False

1. T
2. F
3. F
4. T
5. F

Multiple Choice

1. c
2. c
3. d
4. a
5. c
6. b
7. d
8. d

Activity 9-1   Creating an Alphabetic Index

Record #	Name or Subject	Code 1	Code 2	Code 3
2	Burrows Caroline Mrs	711	40	298
4	Hillcrest Tower Apartments	277	04	332
3	Johnson Anu S Ms	901	22	101
1	Maintenance Records	824	61	375
10	Office Supplies	133	71	390
7	Sams Video Rentals	810	33	274
9	Southwest Designs	401	88	391
8	Vaidyanathan Charla MD	591	28	274
6	VanOettingen Arden Mr	371	55	210
5	Woodland High School	424	92	719

Activity 9-2　Sorting for Consecutive Numeric Storage

1. 10 _____

2. 4 _____

3. 6 _____

4. 9 _____

5. 5 _____

6. 8 _____

7. 2 _____

8. 7 _____

9. 1 _____

10. 3 _____

Activity 9-3　Sorting for Terminal-Digit Storage

1. 3 _____

2. 6 _____

3. 8 _____

4. 7 _____

5. 2 _____

6. 4 _____

7. 1 _____

8. 10 _____

9. 9 _____

10. 5 _____

Activity 9-4　Sorting for Middle-Digit Storage

1. 4 _____

2. 3 _____

3. 8 _____

4. 7 _____

5. 2 _____

6. 6 _____

7. 1 _____

8. 10 _____

9. 9 _____

10. 5 _____

GEOGRAPHIC RECORDS MANAGEMENT

Terms

Directions: Fill in the missing word(s) in the space provided at the left.

1. _____

2. _____

3. _____

4. _____

5. _____

6. _____

7. _____

8. _____

9. _____

10. _____

11. _____

12. _____

1. A(n) _____ is a special guide that serves as a permanent marker in storage indicating that all records pertaining to a particular name are stored in a different location.

2. The _____ is an alphabetic arrangement of major geographic divisions plus one or more geographic subdivisions, also arranged in alphabetic order.

3. A(n) _____ is a computer system designed to allow users to collect, manage, and analyze large volumes of data referenced to a geographic location by some type of geographic coordinates such as longitude and latitude.

4. A method of storing and retrieving records by location using a geographic filing system is called _____.

5. A notation on a folder tab or sheet of paper that directs the filer to multiple locations for related information is a(n) _____.

6. A(n) _____ is the classification of records by geographic location usually arranged by numeric code or in alphabetic order.

7. A sheet placed in an alternate file location that directs the filer to a specific record stored in a different location is a(n) _____.

8. A(n) _____ is any of 32 horizontal directions indicated on the card of a compass.

9. The _____ is a single alphabetic arrangement in which all types of entries (names, subjects, titles, etc.) are interfiled.

10. An arrangement of geographic records with primary guides labeled with alphabetic letters is a(n) _____.

11. A compass point used as part of a company or subject name is a(n) _____.

12. An arrangement of geographic records with primary guides labeled with location names is a(n) _____.

True/False

Directions: Circle T if the statement is true; circle F if the statement is false.

T   F   1. An alphabetic index is not necessary in geographic records storage.

T   F   2. When filing records with compass point terms, each word or unit in a filing segment containing compass terms is considered a separate filing unit.

T   F   3. Geographic records management is important for business activities spanning wide geographic areas that demand intelligent business decisions based on location.

T   F   4. Requests for a record stored by geographic arrangement may identify it by location, by numeric file code, or by the correspondent's name.

T   F   5. Finding property ownership, responding to emergencies, or issuing building permits is slower and less efficient when the records are arranged by location.

T   F   6. One advantage of geographic records storage is its simplicity of design that takes less time to establish than an alphabetic name file.

T   F   7. Geographic storage lacks flexibility for expansion because records are difficult to rearrange.

T   F   8. A geographic arrangement of records that has a small volume of diverse records should use a dictionary arrangement with a location name guide plan.

T   F   9. To maintain a geographically organized file of technical studies conducted by geologists, the compass term is treated as an adjective and is filed after the name.

T   F   10. A SEE ALSO cross-reference notation is used to direct filers to multiple file locations for related information.

Multiple Choice

Directions: Circle the letter of the best answer.

1. Types of cross-references used in geographic records storage include
    a. cross-reference sheets.
    b. cross-reference guides.
    c. cross-reference folders.
    d. both a and b.

2. In a geographic file arranged by state and then city, you would file a letter from a company that does not have an individual or city folder in the file in a(n)
    a. alphabetic name file.
    b. newly prepared individual folder.
    c. general state folder.
    d. newly prepared special city folder.

3. In a geographic file arranged by state and then city, the guide plan is a
    a. location name guide plan.
    b. a lettered guide plan.
    c. a dictionary arrangement.
    d. both a and c.

4. Many geographic filing systems are used to support an internal
    a. geographic internal system.
    b. geographic information system.
    c. geography information service.
    d. geographic implementation system.

5. Which of the following steps are used to remove a record from geographic storage?
    a. Find it, charge it out, follow up on it, and request it.
    b. Charge it out, follow up on it, request it, and find it.
    c. Follow up on it, request it, find it, and charge it out.
    d. Request it, find and remove it, charge it out, and follow up on it.

6. Which of the following steps are used to store records in a geographic file?
    a. Inspect, index, code, cross-reference, sort, and store.
    b. Index, cross-reference, sort, code, store, and inspect.
    c. Inspect, code, index, cross-reference, sort, and store.
    d. Code, cross-reference, and store.

7. The alphabetic index is consulted to see if the correspondent is currently in the system after
    a. coding a document.
    b. inspecting a document.
    c. cross-referencing a document.
    d. none of the above.

8. In geographic storage that uses A–Z as the primary guides and countries as subdivisions, records are stored using a(n)
    a. numeric records storage system.
    b. location name guide plan.
    c. lettered guide plan.
    d. none of the above.

9. When a foreign country name is translated into its English equivalent, a cross-reference to _____ is required.
    a. the native language
    b. a special dictionary
    c. other countries
    d. a different alphabet

10. When filing records with compass point terms for a scientific study, each word or unit in a filing segment containing compass terms is
    a. abbreviated.
    b. treated as an adjective and placed after the name.
    c. a global record.
    d. disregarded.

Matching

Directions: Write the letter of the term that matches each statement in the blank beside each statement below.

      a. cross-reference sheet
      b. numeric file list
      c. SEE ALSO cross-reference
      d. lettered guide plan
      e. location name guide plan

_____ 1. A serial list of the numbers assigned to records in a numeric storage system

_____ 2. A notation on folder tabs or sheets that direct the filer to multiple locations for related information

_____ 3. An arrangement of geographic records that labels primary guides with location names

_____ 4. A sheet placed in an alternate file location that directs the filer to a specific record stored in a different location

_____ 5. An arrangement of geographic records that labels primary guides with alphabetic letters

Short Answer

Directions: Write your response in the space following each question.

1. What determines the primary division in a geographic records management system?

_____

_____

_____

_____

2. Compare and contrast geographic records management with subject records management.

_____

_____

_____

_____

Activity 10-1   Determining Geographic Guides and Folders

Directions: Ski Villages International operates ski resorts in seven countries. You have been asked to give your opinion regarding guides and folders to be used for these properties.

- Review the names and locations of the resorts shown below.

- Then answer the three questions regarding records management for Ski Villages International.

Alpine Ski Village, Aosta, Italy
Rocky Top Chalet, Aspen, USA
Alpine Ski Village, Chamonix, France
Ski Hi Resort and Spa, Cardona, New Zealand
Overlook Lodge, Chamonix, France
Ski Hi Resort and Spa, Innsbruck, Austria
Tyrolean Roost, Kitzbühel, Austria
Bavarian Inn, Garmisch, Germany
Ski Bavaria Resort, Füssen, Germany
Whiteface Mountain Resort, Lake Placid, USA
Edelweiss Hotel, Zermatt, Switzerland

1. Guides and Folders
   a. What primary guide labels should be used in a geographic location name guide plan?

   _____

   _____

   b. Are secondary guides needed?

   _____

   _____

   _____

   c. What would be keyed on the folder labels?

   _____

   _____

   _____

2. Justify your choice by explaining your decisions from Step 1.

_____

_____

_____

_____

_____

3. What cross-references are needed?

_____

_____

_____

_____

Activity 10-2   Creating a Master Index for Geographic Records

Directions: You have been asked to create a master index for the records of Ski Villages International.

1. Prepare a master index, including appropriate cross-references, for the records of Ski Villages International shown in Activity 10-1 on the previous page.

2. Print a copy of the master index.

Activity 10-3   Geographic File Drawer Arrangement

Directions: Identify the guide and folder tab cuts and their file drawer positions in the following portion of a file drawer arrangement.

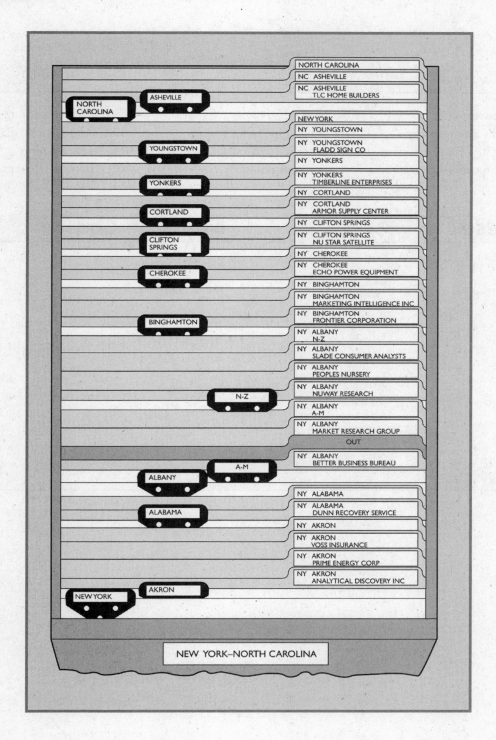

Tab Cut   _____   _____   _____   _____

Guide or Folder Position   _____   _____   _____   _____

SOLUTIONS

Terms

1. cross-reference guide
2. encyclopedic arrangement
3. geographic information system
4. geographic records management
5. SEE ALSO cross-reference
6. geographic filing system
7. cross-reference sheet
8. compass point
9. dictionary arrangement
10. lettered guide plan
11. compass term
12. location name guide plan

True/False

1. F
2. T
3. T
4. T
5. F
6. F
7. F
8. T
9. T
10. T

Multiple Choice

1. d
2. c
3. a
4. b
5. d
6. a
7. a
8. c
9. a
10. b

Matching

1. b
2. c
3. e
4. a
5. d

Short Answer

1. The primary division in a geographic records management system is determined by the volume of records and by the geographic division (country, state or province, city, or other location) by which a record is likely to be requested.

2. Both geographic and subject records management are alphabetic records systems. Geographic records management can also be a numeric records system, and both systems use either a dictionary or encyclopedic arrangement of records. In addition, a master index is prepared for both systems.

   The two systems differ in that arrangement of records in a subject system is by subject category and then name; but in a geographic system, records are arranged first by location and then by name or subject.

Activity 10-1   Determining Geographic Guides and Folders

1. a. The country name should be on primary guide labels.

   b. No secondary guides are needed.

   c. Folder labels would identify the country, the name of the resort, and the city.

2. a. Filers are most likely to remember and request records first by country rather than city names. Therefore, the country name would be on the primary guides.

   b. The limited number of locations makes secondary guides unnecessary.

   c. Folder labels would be prepared based on the decisions made in a and b.

3. A SEE ALSO cross-reference would be prepared for Alpine Ski Village and Ski Hi Resort and Spa because the same name is used for multiple locations. The cross-reference would list the country first and then the city.

Activity 10-2   Creating a Master Index for Geographic Records

Country	City	Indexed Name	See Also
Austria	Innsbruck	Ski Hi Resort and Spa	New Zealand Cardona
Austria	Kitzbühel	Tyrolean Roost	
France	Chamonix	Alpine Ski Village	Italy Aosta
France	Chamonix	Overlook Lodge	
Germany	Füssen	Ski Bavaria Resort	
Germany	Garmisch	Bavarian Inn	
Italy	Aosta	Alpine Ski Village	France Chamonix
New Zealand	Cardona	Ski Hi Resort and Spa	Austria Innsbruck
Switzerland	Zermatt	Edelweiss Hotel	
USA	Aspen	Rocky Top Chalet	
USA	Lake Placid	Whiteface Mountain Resort	

Activity 10-3   Geographic File Drawer Arrangement

Tab Cut: one-fifth, one-fifth, one-fifth, one-third
Guide or Folder Position: first, second, third, fourth

ELECTRONIC AND IMAGE RECORDS

Terms

Directions: Fill in the missing word(s) in the space provided at the left.

1. _____

1. A record stored on electronic storage media that can be readily accessed or changed is a(n) _____.

2. _____

2. _____ is machine-reading of printed or written characters through the use of light-sensitive materials or devices.

3. _____

3. A(n) _____ is a computer program that replicates itself into other programs that are shared among systems with the intention of causing damage.

4. _____

4. _____ technology automatically delivers e-mail and other data to a device based on the user's profile and request for specific data.

5. _____

5. A string of characters known to the computer system and a user, who must specify it to gain access to the system, is a(n) _____.

6. _____

6. The process of moving data from one electronic system to another without re-inputting the data is called _____.

7. _____

7. A(n) _____ drive consists of a small printed circuit board encased in a hard plastic covering.

8. _____

8. _____ are a variety of magnetically coated materials used by computers for data storage.

9. _____

9. A high-density information storage medium where digitally encoded information is both written and read by means of a laser is _____.

10. _____

10. A(n) _____ converts an image of a document to electronic form for processing and storing.

11. _____

11. The process of converting meaningful information into a numeric code that is understood only by the intended recipient of the information is called _____.

12. _____

12. A collection of data designed to support management decision making is a(n) _____.

13. _____

13. A string of characters and numbers added as a code on electronic documents being transmitted by computer is called a(n) _____.

14. _____

14. _____ is how well the media and the equipment needed to access information stored on the media work together.

15. _____

15. A combination hardware and software buffer between an internal network and the Internet to protect the network from outside intrusion is a(n) _____.

16. _____

16. _____ is the length of time the media will maintain its original quality so that it can continue to be used.

17. _____

17. A(n) _____ is a device that allows two or more USB devices to be plugged in via one USB computer port.

18. _____

18. Data that describes other data, its format, and its use is called _____.

19. _____

19. In microfilming, the term _____ refers to the sharpness or fine detail in an image.

20. _____

20. _____ is the degree of opacity of microfilm that determines the amount of light that will pass through it or reflect from it.

21. _____

21. A term that refers to the relationship between the dimensions of the original record and the corresponding dimensions of the microimage is called _____.

22. _____

22. A(n) _____ is a photographic or digital representation of a record on any medium such as microfilm or optical disk.

23. _____

23. The relationship between the size of an image and the original when viewed on a microfilm reader screen is the _____.

24. _____

24. A(n) _____ is a term for any medium containing miniaturized images, or microimages.

25. _____

25. The technology by which recorded information can be quickly reduced to a microform is called _____.

26. _____

26. A(n) _____ requires an individual requesting data from a computer system to make a telephone request, hang up, and wait for the computer to call back.

27. _____

27. _____ is a coding system consisting of vertical lines or bars set in a predetermined pattern that, when read by an optical reader, can be converted into machine-readable language.

28. _____

28. Recording information to serve as a location directory for microforms or electronic records is referred to as _____.

True/False

Directions: Circle T if the statement is true; circle F if the statement is false.

T F 1. Electronic media are magnetic media and optical media.

T F 2. Electronic records may contain quantitative data, text, and images (but not sounds) that originate as an electronic signal.

T F 3. A computer program created to destroy or damage computer data is called a virus.

T F 4. Microrecords must be enlarged and projected onto a viewing screen to be read.

T F 5. Roll film is a unitized microform.

T F 6. Bar codes may be used to help automate the indexing for scanned or microfilmed documents.

Multiple Choice

Directions: Circle the letter of the best answer.

1. Which of the following is an electronic records retention problem?
   a. Passwords
   b. Duplicate records
   c. Employee bonding
   d. Scanners

2. Which of the following does not contain electronic records?
   a. Magnetic tape
   b. CD-ROM
   c. Printed index of storage system
   d. Optical disk

3. Which of the following is an advantage of using removable media?
   a. Removable disks can be used in another system.
   b. Removable disks cannot be used for backup.
   c. If a removable hard drive fails, nothing can be done about it.
   d. Removable hard drives can support only a limited number of disks.

4. The most inexpensive and widely used microform is
   a. microfiche.
   b. the aperture card.
   c. roll film.
   d. the jacket.

5. Which of the following environmental conditions must be controlled during long-term retention storage of microrecords?
   a. Humidity
   b. Light
   c. Temperature
   d. All the above

6. Which of the following magnetic media is a long strip of film coated with magnetizable recording material used for storing information in the form of electromagnetic signals?
   a. Videotape
   b. RAID
   c. Magnetic tape
   d. None of the above

7. Which of the following is a type of technology that automatically delivers e-mail and other data to a device based on the user's profile and request for specific data?
   a. Push
   b. Flash
   c. OCR
   d. RFID

8. Which of the following is NOT an advantage of using hard drives as removable storage?
   a. Removable media can be stored in locked cabinets, vaults, or other secure locations to prevent unauthorized access.
   b. Removable disks can be used in other computer systems with compatible drives.
   c. Removable media are read-only devices that attach to a computer and are usable as a standard hard drive.
   d. Removable disks can be used to back up conventional hard drives and to restore electronic records if a hard drive fails.

Activity 11-1   Visible Electronic Media Labels

Directions: List information that should be included on labels for CDs, DVDs, and other removable storage devices.

1. _____

2. _____

3. _____

4. _____

5. _____

Activity 11-2   Electronic Records Issues

Directions: Answer the following questions.

1. How are computer records indexed?

    _____

    _____

    _____

    _____

2. How are computer records retrieved?

    _____

    _____

    _____

    _____

3. Why is media compatibility a records retention issue?

    _____

    _____

    _____

    _____

4. Why is media stability a records retention issue?

    _____

    _____

    _____

5. Where are active electronic records stored?

_____

_____

_____

_____

6. What is the legal status of a digital signature, or e-signature?

_____

_____

_____

_____

Activity 11-3   Image Records Issues

Directions: Complete the following items as directed.

1. List two reasons for using microforms.

a. _____

_____

b. _____

_____

2. How are documents prepared for microfilming?

_____

_____

_____

_____

3. What records are filmed with the following microfilm cameras?

   a. Rotary camera _____

   b. Planetary camera _____

   c. Step-and-repeat camera _____

   d. Aperture card camera _____

4. Explain what *generation* means as related to microforms.

   _____

   _____

   _____

   _____

5. Why are vital and archival records stored on microfilm?

   _____

   _____

   _____

   _____

6. What is a microfilm jacket, and how is it used?

   _____

   _____

   _____

   _____

7. What are the three stages of an image system?

   _____

   _____

   _____

   _____

Activity 11-4   Electronic and Image Records Index

Directions: You have been asked to create an index of contractors used by the South Hampton Mall.

1. Create an *Access* database named *SG Activity 11-4.*

2. Create a table named **Index for Contractors SH Mall 02-10.** Include the following fields in the table: Record ID, Contractor Name, Record Date, Media, Location, Retention Period, and Total Retention. Make Record ID an AutoNumber field and the primary key. Make all other fields text fields.

3. Enter data for the records shown below.

4. Sort the table by the Contractor Name field in ascending order.

5. Print the database table.

Records for 11-4						
Record ID	**Contractor Name**	**Record Date**	**Media**	**Location**	**Retention Period**	**Total Retention**
1	Advanced Concrete Systems	05-24-2009	Microfilm	Active	5 yrs.	P
2	Parking Lot Specialists	06-06-2007	Hard Drive	Active	1 yr.	P
3	Forrest Equipment Rentals	01-12-2010	Hard Drive	Active	5 yrs.	P
4	Giovanetti Engineering Associates	03-04-2010	Aperture Card	Active	2 yrs.	P
5	United-Krauss Signs, Inc.	05-05-2007	Hard Drive	Offsite	5 yrs.	10 yrs.
6	Viasoft Security Systems	10-31-2008	DVD	Active	2 yrs.	5 yrs.

Activity 11-5   Electronic Records Storage Research

Directions: Complete this activity to learn more about storing records electronically.

1. Use your favorite search engine to search the Internet for information on electronic records storage. Information may include types of storage media discussed in Chapter 11, environmental issues regarding electronic records storage, security issues, or general usage recommendations. Use search terms such as *electronic records storage, electronic records storage media, storage environment for electronic records,* or a related term of your choice.

2. Select an article that you find based on your search and write a brief summary of it.

SOLUTIONS

Terms

1. electronic record
2. optical character recognition (OCR)
3. virus
4. push
5. password
6. migration
7. flash
8. magnetic media
9. optical media
10. scanner
11. encryption
12. data warehouse
13. digital signature, electronic signature, or e-signature
14. media compatibility
15. firewall
16. media stability
17. USB hub
18. metadata
19. resolution
20. density
21. reduction ratio
22. image record
23. magnification ratio or enlargement ratio
24. microform
25. micrographics
26. call-back system
27. bar code
28. indexing

True/False

1. T
2. F
3. T
4. T
5. F
6. T

Multiple Choice

1. b
2. c
3. a
4. c
5. d
6. c
7. a
8. c

Activity 11-1   Visible Electronic Media Labels

1. Department, unit, or organization that created the records
2. Name of records series
3. Inclusive dates, numeric series, or other identifying information
4. Type of computer on which the records were created
5. Software name and version used to create the records

Activity 11-2   Electronic Records Issues

1. Indexing computer-based records involves fields and keywords. It is the mental process of deciding the name or code by which a record will be stored and retrieved. A record identifier code or filename is entered to code each record. Multiple levels of folders, or directories and subdirectories, help organize computer-stored records. If full-text indexing is used, every word in a document may be used to locate it.

2. With an online index or log of directories, subdirectories, and filenames, users can locate and retrieve all electronic records. Visible electronic records are retrieved by locating desired records that are properly labeled. Files in large tape libraries are located by using an index and directing software to guide a robotic arm to retrieve a tape.

3. Media compatibility refers to how well the media and the equipment needed to access information stored on the media work together. Older media may not work on newer equipment. Current media may not work on future equipment.

4. Because media and equipment are manufactured with planned obsolescence in mind, data created on older media, software, operating systems, and equipment need to be migrated to other media for long-term retention. State-of-the-art technology is replaced by newer state-of-the art technology, sometimes very quickly. The stable life expectancy of electronic records is often shorter than the required retention period for the information stored on the media.

5. The most active electronic records are stored near the user in easily accessible equipment. They may be inside a computer on a hard drive or on removable storage devices such as CDs and DVDs. They also may be stored in desktop storage boxes, media pages, or towers.

6. The Electronics Signature in Global and National Commerce Act, passed in 2000, sets national standards for electronic signatures and records and gives them the same legal validity as written contracts and documents. The law provides that no contract, signature, or record shall be denied legally binding status just because it is in electronic form.

Activity 11-3   Image Records Issues

1. Students may list any two of the following reasons for using microforms:
   a. They contain one unit of information.
   b. They provide compact storage.
   c. They reduce storage space requirements.
2. Records must be removed from file cabinets or other containers and folders and stacked neatly in correct sequence. All paper clips and staples must be removed, torn pages mended, and all attachments removed.
3. a. A rotary camera is used for filming large-volume records such as checks and invoices.
   b. A planetary camera is used for filming large engineering drawings, hardbound books, and other large documents.
   c. A step-and-repeat camera is used for filming any records to be stored on microfiche.
   d. An aperture card camera is used for filming engineering drawings or other large source documents.
4. *Generation* indicates the relationship of a copy to the original source document. First-generation microforms are camera-original microforms. Second-generation microforms are copies made from camera-original microforms. Third-generation microforms are copies of copies, and so on.
5. Vital and archival records are often stored on microfilm because of its durability. The standardized format of microfilm protects records from technological obsolescence. Microfilm needs only projection and magnification for reading, and microfilm is admissible as evidence in court.
6. A microfilm jacket is a flat, transparent, plastic carrier made to hold single or multiple film strips. A jacket has one or more sleeves or channels for inserting and protecting strips of 16-mm or 35-mm microfilm. Jackets can be updated by inserting new microfilm into a channel. Jackets keep related records together.
7. The three stages of an image system are:
   - Preparation
   - Processing
   - Use

Activity 11-4   Electronic and Image Records Index

Index for Contractors SH Mall 02-10 Table

Index for Contractors SH Mall 02-10						
Record ID	Contractor Name	Record Date	Media	Location	Retention Period	Total Retention
1	Advanced Concrete Systems	05/24/2009	Microfilm	Active	5 yrs.	P
3	Forrest Equipment Rentals	01/12/2010	Hard Drive	Active	5 yrs.	P
4	Giovanetti Engineering Associates	03/04/2010	Aperture Card	Active	2 yrs.	P
2	Parking Lot Specialists	06/06/2007	Hard Drive	Active	1 yr.	P
5	United-Krauss Signs, Inc.	05/05/2007	Hard Drive	Offsite	5 yrs.	10 yrs.
6	Viasoft Security Systems	10/31/2008	DVD	Active	2 yrs.	5 yrs.

THE RECORDS AND INFORMATION MANAGEMENT PROGRAM

Terms

Directions: Fill in the missing word(s) in the space provided at the left.

1. _____

2. _____

3. _____

4. _____

5. _____

6. _____

7. _____

8. _____

9. _____

10. _____

1. A(n) _____ is a sudden emergency event that results in major loss of resources or disruption of operations for an organization.

2. _____ involves necessary activities to restore operations quickly.

3. A(n) _____ has a fixed arrangement of predetermined spaces designed for entering and extracting prescribed information on a physical or electronic document.

4. _____ knowledge is acquired through practice.

5. Data that are preprinted on a form and do not require rewriting each time the form is filled in is _____ data.

6. A pre-assembled set of forms glued together at the top is a(n) _____.

7. A(n) _____ plan is a written and approved course of action to take when disaster strikes, ensuring an organization's ability to respond to an interruption in services by restoring critical business functions.

8. A(n) _____ is a periodic inspection to verify that an operation is in compliance with a records and information management program.

9. _____ data change each time a form is filled in.

10. _____ is an interdisciplinary field concerned with systematic, effective management and use of an organization's knowledge resources, including the knowledge and experience of its employees.

True/False

Directions: Circle T if the statement is true; circle F if the statement is false.

T   F   1. A forms designer needs to know the type of items to be filled in and their sequence.

T   F   2. Standardized business forms provide an efficient means for gathering a great deal of needed information.

T   F   3. A destructive fire is not considered to be a disaster.

T   F   4. A disaster recovery plan provides for the restoration of records but not equipment and personnel.

T   F   5. An organization in compliance follows federal laws and regulations, but it does not have to follow any state laws.

Multiple Choice

Directions: Circle the letter of the best answer.

1. Data that change each time a form is filled in are
   a. unnecessary data.
   b. variable data.
   c. constant data.
   d. important data.

2. A telephone message form can be a(n)
   a. electronic form.
   b. single-copy form.
   c. multiple-copy form.
   d. All the above

3. Which of the following types of information are obtained through a records audit?
   a. Recommendations for improving the RIM program
   b. Information about current operations
   c. An analysis of the current system
   d. All the above

4. When an unforeseen event occurs, employees need to
   a. grab their personal belongings and leave the building.
   b. wait until someone tells them what to do.
   c. take immediate action to avoid loss or disruption of operations.
   d. None of the above

5. The highest cost of operating records and information management programs is in
   a. labor costs.
   b. space utilization costs.
   c. equipment costs.
   d. supplies costs.

6. Which of the following are components of a RIM program?
   a. Records storage
   b. Records retention and destruction
   c. Compliance
   d. All of the above

7. Which of the following terms is also used to describe vital records?
   a. Essential records
   b. Mission-critical records
   c. Long-term records
   d. Very important records

Activity 12-1   Summary of Chapter Contents

1. List four components of a RIM program.

   a. _____

   b. _____

   c. _____

   d. _____

2. List three RIM program responsibilities.

   a. _____

   b. _____

   c. _____

3. List five retention implementation actions.

   a. _____

   b. _____

   c. _____

   d. _____

   e. _____

4. List three cost control measures that may be undertaken to control the costs of equipment, space, salaries, and supplies.

   a. _____

   b. _____

   c. _____

5. List five sections included in a typical records and information manual.

   a. _____

   b. _____

   c. _____

   d. _____

   e. _____

6. List three kinds of information about a records and information management program that a records audit provides.

   a. _____

   b. _____

   c. _____

7. List six goals of forms management.

   a. _____

   b. _____

   c. _____

   d. _____

   e. _____

   f. _____

Activity 12-2   Designing a Seminar Registration Form

Directions: You have been asked to use Word to prepare a registration form for a health and wellness seminar to be held at your school this evening at 7:30 p.m.

1. Plan your form in the space below before you begin to design it on the computer.

2. Include a form number and revision date. Include the following information on your form.
   - Name of your school
   - Title of the form: *Health and Wellness Seminar Registration*
   - Date and time of the seminar

3. Include the following instructions: *Please use one form per person. Fill out all information.*

4. Include the following constant data: *Name, Address, City, State, ZIP Code, Telephone No., E-mail Address, School Name, Campus,* and *Class* (Options: *Freshman, Sophomore, Junior, Senior,* and *Other*).

Activity 12-3   Evaluating the Files

Directions: You are a records clerk in the office of Brighthouse Condominium Management Corporation. While examining the files, you find the problems listed in the left column of the table below. Indicate in the right column the standard that should be applied to control each problem. (Suggestion: Carefully check Chapter 12 as well as other related chapters of your textbook to complete this activity.)

File Problem	Standard to Apply to Correct the Problem
EXAMPLE: All file drawers are packed with folders.	Allow 3 or 4 inches of working space in each drawer.
1. Many file drawers do not have file guides.	
2. File folders vary in tab size, tab position, and construction (paper weight).	
3. Some folders have labels. Other folders have only a number or letter written on the tab. Some labels are torn or taped to the folder.	
4. About one-third of the folders are overcrowded.	
5. The storage method is alphabetic, but the file drawers are labeled with numbers 1–16 (for the four 4-drawer cabinets).	

SOLUTIONS

Terms

1. disaster
2. recovery
3. form
4. tacit
5. constant
6. multicopy form
7. disaster recovery
8. records audit
9. variable
10. knowledge management

True/False

1. T
2. T
3. F
4. F
5. F

Multiple Choice

1. b
2. d
3. d
4. c
5. a
6. d
7. b

Activity 12-1   Summary of Chapter Contents

1. Students may list any four of the following RIM program components:
   a. Records storage
   b. Records retention and destruction
   c. Compliance
   d. Active records management
   e. Inactive records management
   f. Vital records protection

2. Students may list any three of the following RIM program responsibilities:
   a. Records audit
   b. Records and information manual
   c. Forms management
   d. Disaster prevention, preparedness, and recovery
   e. Knowledge management
   f. RIM software
   g. Policy implementation and enforcement
3. All of the following are retention implementation actions:
   a. Identify records series eligible for retention actions.
   b. Destroy records with elapsed retention periods.
   c. Transfer inactive paper or photographic records to offsite storage.
   d. Transfer inactive electronic records from hard drives to removable media for offline or offsite storage.
   e. Destroy physical copies after records are microfilmed or scanned.
4. All of the following cost control measures may be undertaken to control the costs of equipment, space, salaries, and supplies:
   a. Eliminate unnecessary records.
   b. Supervise the use of equipment and supplies carefully.
   c. Select equipment and media that require less space and less time to operate.
5. Students may list any of the following sections of a typical records and information manual:
   a. RIM program overview
   b. Classification system
   c. Storage procedures for records on all media
   d. Records retention schedules
   e. Storage locations
   f. Annual program evaluation or audit
   g. Records disposition
   h. Disaster recovery plan
   i. RIM software
6. All of the following kinds of information are provided by a records audit:
   a. Information about current operations
   b. Analysis of current system and its needs
   c. Recommended solutions for improving the RIM program
7. All of the following are goals of forms management:
   a. Determine the number and use of forms.
   b. Eliminate unnecessary forms.
   c. Standardize form size, paper quality, typefaces, and design features such as company logos and form numbers.
   d. Ensure efficient form design.
   e. Establish efficient, economical procedures for printing, storing, and distributing forms.
   f. Determine which forms can be completed online.

Activity 12-2   Designing a Seminar Registration Form

Compare your design with the following example. Did you:

- Include the name of your school, the title of the form, and the date and time of the seminar?
- Include necessary instructions?
- Provide adequate space for variable data?
- Use check boxes rather than fill-ins where possible?
- Include a form number and revision date?

(NAME OF YOUR SCHOOL)

HEALTH AND WELLNESS SEMINAR REGISTRATION

(Current Date)
7:30 p.m.

Please use one form per person. Fill out all information.

Name	Address	City
State	ZIP Code	Telephone No.
E-mail Address	School Name	Campus

Class
☐ Freshman   ☐ Sophomore   ☐ Junior   ☐ Senior   ☐ Other

Form RM 123 (Rev. 07/09)

Activity 12-3   Evaluating the Files

Standards to apply to correct the problem:

File Problem	Standard to Apply to Correct the Problem
EXAMPLE: All file drawers are packed with folders.	Allow 3 or 4 inches of working space in each drawer.
1. Many file drawers do not have any file guides.	1. Provide 10–15 file guides per file drawer.
2. File folders vary in tab size, tab position, and construction (paper weight).	2. Use uniform folders (tab style and size, weight of folder stock) throughout the drawers.
3. Some folders have labels. Other folders have only a number or letter written on the tab. Some labels are torn or taped to the folder.	3. Use uniform size and style of labels, with uniform, readable typefaces. Replace labels when they will no longer stay on the folder.
4. About one-third of the folders are overcrowded.	4. No more than 3/4" of material should be stored in folders.
5. The storage method is alphabetic, but the file drawers are labeled with numbers 1–16 (for the four 4-drawer cabinets).	5. Label folders alphabetically according to folder content and drawer content range.